FREUD/LYNCH

FREUD/LYNCH
Behind the Curtain

Edited by

Jamie Ruers and Stefan Marianski

First published in 2023 by
Phoenix Publishing House Ltd
62 Bucknell Road
Bicester
Oxfordshire OX26 2DS

British Library Cataloguing in Publication Data

A C.I.P. for this book is available from the British Library

ISBN-13: 978-1-912691-95-1

Typeset by Medlar Publishing Solutions Pvt Ltd, India

www.firingthemind.com

Contents

Acknowledgements

The editors wish to express their thanks to Kate Pearce and Fernando Marques of Phoenix Publishing House for their tireless support and endless patience, to the wonderful teams at the Rio Cinema and the Freud Museum, to Karolina Heller for her exquisite poster and cover designs, to David Lynch for kindly granting his permission to reproduce his artworks, to the BFI for permission to use its images, to our contributors, and to everyone who attended the conference.

About the editors and contributors

Olga Cox Cameron's first career was in literary studies, having written an MA thesis on Proust, worked as a tutor in the Department of French at University College, Dublin, and started—but not completed—a PhD on Beckett at the University of Fribourg in Switzerland. Following a decade of working with homeless people in Dublin, she trained as a psychoanalyst at St Vincent's University Hospital, completed a PhD on narrative (im)possibilities in psychosis, and has been in private practice for the past thirty-three years. She lectured in Psychoanalytic Theory and also in Psychoanalysis and Literature at St Vincent's University Hospital and Trinity College from 1991 to 2013 and has published numerous articles on these topics in national and international journals. She is the founder of the annual Irish Psychoanalysis and Cinema Festival, now in its thirteenth year.

Tamara Dellutri is a Lacanian psychoanalyst from Buenos Aires, Argentina. Ms Dellutri has trained in the field of music, critical theory, and the visual arts. She is a member of the International of the Forums: School of Psychoanalysis of the Forums of the Lacanian Field (IF-SPFLF). Ms Dellutri practices in the UK where she is currently undertaking postgraduate studies in law and public health, with a research interest in Mental Capacity Law.

Allister Mactaggart, PhD, is an independent lecturer, researcher, and writer with a long-standing interest in David Lynch's various creative endeavours. He is the author of *The Film Paintings of David Lynch: Challenging Film Theory* (Intellect, 2010), in addition to which he has published on landscapes in Lynch's work in relation to the legacy of the sublime in North American art, on pop music and loss in *Mulholland Drive*, and on the significance of photography in *Twin Peaks: The Return*.

Stefan Marianski is Education Manager at the Freud Museum London, where he works to engage young people with psychoanalytic thought. He has organised a number of events and conferences on psychoanalytic themes, and has written and lectured on dreams, sexuality, anthropology, surrealism, and masculinity. He is a member of the Psychosis Therapy Project and a trainee at the Centre for Freudian Analysis and Research.

Richard Martin is Director of Education and Public Programmes at Whitechapel Gallery, and a tutor at UCL's Bartlett School of Architecture. He was previously Curator, Public Programmes at Tate. Richard is the author of *The Architecture of David Lynch* (Bloomsbury, 2014) and he organised the 2009 symposium 'Mapping the Lost Highway: New Perspectives on David Lynch' held at Tate Modern. He completed his PhD at the London Consortium and has also taught at Birkbeck, University of London, Middlesex University, and King's College London.

Todd McGowan teaches theory and film at the University of Vermont. He is the author of *Universality and Identity Politics* (Columbia, 2020), *Emancipation After Hegel* (Columbia, 2021), *Only a Joke Can Save Us* (Northwestern, 2017), *Capitalism and Desire* (Columbia, 2016), and other works. He is the co-editor of the Diaeresis series at Northwestern University Press (with Slavoj Žižek and Adrian Johnston) and the editor of the Film Theory in Practice series at Bloomsbury.

Carol Owens is a psychoanalyst and clinical supervisor in private practice in Dublin. She has edited and authored a number of publications in the field of Lacanian psychoanalysis, most recently *Psychoanalysing Ambivalence with Freud and Lacan: On and Off the Couch* with Stephanie Swales (Routledge, 2019). She is series editor for Studying Lacan's Seminars published by Routledge.

Chris Rodley, at the age of six, decided he wanted to be an artist. He graduated in Fine Art (Painting) in 1974, and then in 1976 with a Postgraduate Art Teaching Degree. Having become disillusioned with his painting, horrified by his experience of teaching, but now completely obsessed with the movies, he began programming independent cinemas in 1977, and was Co-Director of Cinema at the Institute of Contemporary Arts in London from 1979–1984. Courtesy of Channel Four, he was able to begin making documentaries in 1983 and he has been an independent filmmaker ever since. In the intervening thirty-five years he has produced and/or directed over eighty arts documentaries for television and contributed to over a dozen documentary series. These include award-winning films on Andy Warhol and Johnny Cash, as well as the series *The Genius of Photography* and *This is Modern Art.* He first worked with David Lynch in 1993 while making a documentary about American independent cinema. In 1996 he spent some time on the set of Lynch's *Lost Highway* and made a short film for the BBC about its making and meaning. That year he and Lynch also began working on the book *Lynch on Lynch* (Faber & Faber, 1997), which has since been updated (Farrar, Straus and Giroux, 2005). He also worked extensively with the director David Cronenberg, making two documentaries about his work (one in 1986 and one in 1992), as well as editing the book *Cronenberg on Cronenberg* (Faber & Faber, 1996) based on years of recorded interviews. Unlike David Lynch, he never returned to painting—David really told him off about that.

Jamie Ruers is Events Manager at the Freud Museum London, where she builds a public programme of events, conferences, and exhibitions that engage with psychoanalysis through a range of disciplines. She is an art historian whose research focuses on various cultural aspects of Vienna in the nineteenth- and twentieth-centuries, and Surrealist art, fashion and film. She has published and lectured for organisations around the world, including the Victoria & Albert Museum, the Argentine Psychoanalytic Association, the Chilean Psychoanalytic Association and the Austrian Cultural Forum and Arts Fund.

Andrea Sabbadini is Fellow of the British Psychoanalytical Society and its former Director of Publications. He works in private practice in London, is Honorary Senior Lecturer at University College London (UCL), Consultant to the IPA in Culture Committee, founder editor of the journal *Psychoanalysis and History*, founder and former Director of the European Psychoanalytic Film Festival (EPFF), and former trustee of the Freud Museum London. His books include *Boundaries and Bridges: Perspectives on Time and Space in Psychoanalysis* (Karnac, 2014) and *Moving Images: Psychoanalytic Reflections on Film* (Routledge, 2014).

Mary Wild is the creator of the PROJECTIONS lecture series at the Freud Museum London, applying psychoanalysis to film interpretation. Her interests include surrealism, the horror genre, auteur studies, and cinematic representations of mental illness.

Introduction

Jamie Ruers and Stefan Marianski

This book collects together many of the papers given at the Freud Museum London's conference, "Freud/Lynch: Behind the Curtain". Over a sunny May weekend, fans, cinephiles, scholars, and psychoanalysts descended on Dalston in East London to ponder the wonderful and strange work of David Lynch. Held in the intense, uncanny atmosphere of the Rio Cinema, a venue eerily reminiscent of *Mulholland Drive*'s (2001) Club Silencio, the conference was abuzz with excitement. Animated discussions filled the auditorium, mingling in the foyer with the aromas of damn fine coffee before spilling out onto the street, so that any passers-by catching a few fragments of conversation about the mysteries of Lumberton, the sinister underbelly of Twin Peaks, or the depravity of Bobby Peru could be forgiven for surmising that it was a convention of detectives (or perverts).

Freud/Lynch

As organisers of the conference—and editors of the present volume—we were excited at the prospect of putting the shrink from Vienna into dialogue with the Eagle Scout from Missoula, but also aware of the potential sensitivities of doing so. Like the taste sensation when maple syrup collides with ham, the combination Freud/Lynch would be appealing to some but repellent to others, particularly those sympathetic to the latter's notorious reticence about the meaning of his works and aversion to reductive explanatory frameworks. Lynch, who famously walked out of his first and only session with a "psychiatrist" upon being told that the therapeutic work could damage his creativity (Lynch, 2007, p. 61), prizes the creative act of producing filmic worlds above all else, placing the onus on his spectators to find their own unique ways of entering into the experience. In his view, trying to "make intellectual sense" of a film comes at the expense of finding "an explanation from within" for which there is no other guide than one's own intuition (ibid. p. 20).

With views like these, it seems likely that Lynch would agree with Freud's famous maxim that "before the problem of the creative artist analysis must, alas, lay down its arms" (Freud, 1928b, p. 177). Yet curiously enough, this turns out to be just one of many ways in which Lynch appears to be in alignment with Freud. While not sharing the latter's technical vocabulary, Lynch's films are replete with Freudian motifs and preoccupations, as is the approach that guides their creation, so much so that many of his accounts of his creative process sound like excellent descriptions of Freud's method of free association: a fragment of an idea comes like a "little fish", and "thinking about that small fragment, that little fish, will bring more, and they'll come in and they'll hook on" (Lynch & Holdengräber, 2014). Lynch figuratively describes these fragments as arriving as if from an "other room" (ibid.), a description strikingly analogous to the famous "other scene" in which Freud locates the unconscious as a psychical locality distinct from consciousness (Freud, 1900a, p. 536).

Lynch's apparent unfamiliarity with Freud makes their common ground all the more intriguing. The conceptual vocabulary of psychoanalysis is notoriously inelegant, but it enables its practitioners to elicit the kinds of dreamlike and often deeply moving subjective compositions that make up the fruits of Lynch's own associative process, to the point that one could even characterise Lynch as a Freudian who has no need for Freud. Chris Rodley, at a time when he was rather more enthusiastic about theory than he is in the present volume, wrote that Freud's account of "the uncanny" (1919h) captures "the essence of

Lynch's cinema" (Rodley, 2005, p. x). Yet in spite of all this, Lynch is by no means a card-carrying Freudian.

Paging Dr Jacoby!

An exchange in the first season of *Twin Peaks* (1990–1991) seems to encapsulate the apparent misalliance between Lynch and Freud:

> *AGENT COOPER: Were her problems of a sexual nature?*
> *DR JACOBY: Agent Cooper, the problems of our entire society are of a sexual nature!*

The response to FBI Special Agent Dale Cooper's (Kyle MacLachlan) question could almost have been lifted from Freud's *Civilization and its Discontents* (1930a), yet it comes from the mouth of eccentric psychiatrist Dr Lawrence Jacoby (Russ Tamblyn), to whom Agent Cooper, and we as spectators, have taken an instant dislike. If Jacoby's rejoinder leaves any room for doubt as to his Freudian inclinations, consider the ensuing conversation, in which he suggests to Cooper that Laura Palmer (Sheryl Lee) suffered from an obscure psychosexual malaise against which she was engaged in a violent defensive struggle—and that her cocaine use was in fact a form of self-medication. Noticing a map of Tibet on the wall, Dr Jacoby proclaims to a po-faced Cooper that

> my abiding interests lie to the east as well. But only as far as Hawaii. The ancient Hawaiians often turned to the soothing rhizome of the ginger plant to ease the pain of profound confusion *which, more often than not, was sexual.*

In a town populated by lovable eccentrics, it is striking that Jacoby's quirks make him conspicuously *un*lovable from his very first appearance, which has him suggestively running his finger under the skirt of the hula dancer on his tie (little wonder the audience of a 1991 episode of *The Phil Donahue Show* voted him most likely to be Laura Palmer's killer). Insinuations of sexual depravity will of course be familiar to those of a psychoanalytic persuasion, for whom the popular caricature of Freud as a "creep" goes hand-in-hand with the irreducibly disturbing nature of his discoveries.

Needless to say, it would be extremely fanciful to ascribe the negative light in which Jacoby is portrayed to some cryptic expression of Lynch's misgivings about Freud. The exchange features in an episode written by Robert Engels under the supervision of Mark Frost and directed by Tim Hunter, and even allowing for Lynch's creative influence, such a contrived subtext would go against everything we know about him as a filmmaker. Nonetheless, with his sexual interests, questionable professional ethics, and permissive attitude towards cocaine, Dr Jacoby is practically a living embodiment of the anti-Freud stereotypes that were in circulation by the 1990s—all the more so when we learn from the official *Twin Peaks* mythology that shortly after Laura Palmer's death his licence to practice was revoked due to his failure to recognise the signs that she had been suffering sexual abuse at the hands of her father (Frost, 2016, p. 333). This indictment resonates with the infamous and widely disputed claims put forward by Masson (1985) that Freud ignored his discovery of widespread sexual abuse within families.

Curious resemblances aside, the exchange between Agent Cooper and Dr Jacoby suggests a deeper incongruity. The latter's Freudian wisecrackery comes across as not only creepy but downright obstructive and, worse still, indicative of a fundamental incompatibility of worldviews. His appeal to common ground serves only to accentuate that his interest in "the east" goes no further than the sexual hang-ups of the ancient Hawaiians, a dubious piece of sexual trivia that calls to mind the local sexual customs of the Bosnian Turks that Freud thinks better of bringing up with a perfect stranger in his famous "Signorelli" parapraxis (1901b, p. 3). Cooper's compassion for the plight of the Tibetan people, on the other hand, is of a seemingly higher dimension: it is bound up with his acquisition of "a deductive technique involving mind-body coordination operating hand-in-hand with the deepest level of intuition". The message seems clear: the closest Twin Peaks has to a resident Freudian is not only uncooperative but—with "apologies in advance for Albert"—un-*Cooper*-ative. Freud and Lynch would thus be as likely bedfellows as Dr Jacoby and Cooper. Of course, if the scene labours to sustain an opposition—a little *too* strenuously, a psychoanalyst might observe—between the squeaky-clean lawman and the licentious shrink, it is one that is far from intact by the end of season two, let alone *Twin Peaks: Fire Walk With Me* (1992), by which time Twin Peaks' primal scene has been laid bare in all its Freudian intensity. But perhaps that's another story. Despite his love of dream logic, one would be hard pressed to imagine Lynch giving his countenance to such a reading.

Behind the curtain

Is there something fundamentally un-Cooper-ative about Freud? Does Freud/Lynch presuppose the reduction of the playful, creative flow of the artist to a set of predefined coordinates? The question was never far from our minds, yet our fidelity was first and foremost not to stultifying theorisations but rather to what we took to be the *spirit* of both Freud and Lynch: a spirit of radical openness to the new and the unexpected, of questioning rather than answering, of opening things up rather than closing them down, and above all of the dialogue. Our subtitle, *Behind the Curtain*, should not be taken to imply that psychoanalysis lays bare what in Lynch's films remain veiled. Our goal was not to fill in what Lynch leaves open, but rather to mobilise these gaps as productive spaces where thought and imagination can be set to work. Few of our contributors would call themselves Freudian, yet each of them is engaged in their own kind of conversation with Lynch. An encounter with Lynch, with Freud, or indeed with one's own unconscious, is always a singular experience.

Chris Rodley opens this volume with a contribution that draws on personal experience. Having interviewed Lynch numerous times, Rodley reflects on their meetings, and particularly on Lynch's reluctance to explain or entertain any specific readings of his work. Lynch's very practice, Rodley notes, is itself "a dreaming process", and dreams are easily trampled. Sceptical of both the auteur theory of the 1940s and 1950s, with its insistence on grounding the work in the author's intentions, and the rise of psychoanalytic film theory in the 1970s, with its search for the unconscious in the text of the film itself, Rodley's chapter might seem an inauspicious start for *Freud/Lynch*. Yet curiously enough, many of his observations—about the limits of language and the artwork's resistance to it, about the material dimension of language that is outside any question of meaning, and about the impossibility of any exhaustive intellectual recuperation of what is at stake in dreams—find remarkable consonance with psychoanalytic thought, as explored in many of the chapters that follow.

What made it possible to describe something as "Lynchian"? Focusing on Lynch not as a person but as a cultural phenomenon, Carol Owens' contribution makes a compelling case for "the Lynchian" as a palimpsest of "the Freudian", drawing on an array of examples from Lynch's works, psychoanalytic theory, popular culture and the clinic, to affirm that "David Lynch doesn't need to be a Freudian for the cultural moment that is 'the Lynchian' to be so". If Rodley warns us of the misguidedness of any attempt to supply the hidden "meaning", Freudian or otherwise, of Lynch's oneiric work, Owens reminds us that such interpretative speculations had little to do with Freud's approach to the workings of the unconscious in the first place. Of particular note is the attention Owens pays to what Freud called the dream's "navel", its "point of contact with the unknown" (Freud, 1900a, p. 525), which resists domestication by language and remains irreducibly disturbing, and which becomes with Lacan the epistemological predicament of speaking beings.

Disturbance is also at the heart of Olga Cox Cameron's contribution, which finds in *Mulholland Drive* a text replete with the mechanisms of the dream-work identified in Freud's *Interpretation of Dreams* (1900a). Placing it alongside James Joyce's *Finnegans Wake* (1939) as rare examples of artworks which succeed in reproducing dream logic, Cox Cameron examines the film with reference to the question posed by Lacan (1991, p. 155) in relation to Freud's famous dream of Irma's injection: given that the dream repeatedly comes up against something that provokes anxiety, what allows the dreamer to continue dreaming? Cox Cameron deftly identifies specific "nevralgic points" at which the film's narrative approaches, then veers away from a traumatic encounter that is distinctly suggestive of the aforementioned "navel", showing how the means it employs to protect the dreamer have the paradoxical effect of staining the entire narrative with its traumatic Freudo-Lynchian nucleus.

Veering away (fittingly) from this line of thought, Mary Wild's contribution is a lyrical homage to Los Angeles. Wild's playful meditation starts out by considering Lynch's own attachment to the City of Angels before going on to ponder its peculiar psycho-geography, finding in its many contrasts and incongruities an apt setting for *Lost Highway* (1997),

Mulholland Drive, and *Inland Empire* (2006). In a wide-ranging exploration that touches on the O. J. Simpson trial, the glamour of the Hollywood dream factory, and the abject darkness of its underside, Wild's chapter takes as its touchstone the notion of "psychogenic fugue". The term, itself a remnant of the era of psychoanalytic psychiatry, is said to have captivated Lynch in the 1990s, and seems to epitomise his ongoing preoccupation with the blurring and fragmentation of identity that are particularly characteristic of this apparent trilogy of LA-based films.

Is Jeffrey Beaumont (Kyle MacLachlan) a detective or a pervert? Both, according to Andrea Sabbadini, whose contribution trenchantly dissects the sinister underbelly of Lumberton in Lynch's *Blue Velvet* (1986). Focusing particularly on the theme of voyeurism, Sabbadini examines how we as spectators become implicated in this "strange world": the identifications the film induces in us as spectators accompanying Jeffrey to the primal scene at the core of his masculinity and identity. While avoiding the usual clichés of reading *Blue Velvet* as a straightforward oedipal fairy tale, Sabbadini's intervention is also of note for deftly bringing out the psychoanalytic significance of the severed ear. Serving as the film's emblematic MacGuffin, this uncanny "part object" is examined not only in terms of the primitive anxieties it evokes but also as a means of initiating us into the oft-overlooked auditory dimensions of Lynch's work and of the inner world.

Lynch's depictions of women are the focus of Jamie Ruers' contribution, which finds surprising points of resonance between his female characters and psychoanalytic understandings of hysteria. Ruers interrogates the "Lynchian hysteric" through a series of remarkable juxtapositions drawn from the history of hysteria, from the ancient notions of "wandering womb" from which the term derives to its modernisations by Charcot and Freud, the fascination of the surrealists, through to Lacan's structural revision with its emphasis on hysteria as a mode of questioning the Other. Touching on themes of desire, trauma, the body, father–daughter relations, and the death drive, Ruers finds in the Lynchian hysteric the subversive embodiment of the incongruities of Lynch's filmic universe.

Stefan Marianski draws on Lacan's interest in the topology of surfaces to propose that *Lost Highway* be investigated topologically. His tentative reading of the film sets out with an examination of the line "Dick Laurent is dead" that both opens and closes the film. The simultaneous sameness and difference of this enigmatic line, Marianski suggests, discloses a constitutive disturbance that determines the film's structure as a surface organised around a hole, another possible parallel with the nevralgic "navel" of the dream. Echoing Rodley's caution about the misuses of interpretation, Marianski opposes approaches that aspire towards an ideal of narrative closure, arguing instead that a properly psychoanalytic reading of the film must take into account the hole as a formal element of constitutive incompleteness and its jouissance effects on the filmic text.

The famous Club Silencio scene from *Mulholland Drive* serves as the point of departure for Allister Mactaggart's contribution, which finds in the Magician's (Richard Green) words "it is an illusion" fertile ground for a reflection on Lynch's creative practice. Navigating a wide array of perspectives on Lynch's philosophical roots. Mactaggart's chapter is also notable for its bold and timely reading of *Twin Peaks: The Return* (2017) as offering a poetic response to the Anthropocene and imminent climate catastrophe. Against the criticism of Lynch as a deliberately incomprehensible trickster, Mactaggart concludes that he is first and foremost a fine artist, "a damn fine artist", whose film and television work must be situated as part of a creative practice that also encompasses painting, photography, design, and music.

At the time of the conference, many of us were still reeling from *Twin Peaks: The Return* the final episode of which had aired just eight months previously. While *The Return* finds its way into most of the chapters in this volume—from Rodley's comments on the celebrated "who is the dreamer?" dream to Ruers' exploration of the tragic fate of Audrey Horner (Sherilyn Fenn), Mactaggart's reflections on episode eight and the Anthropocene, and Marianski's reading of the glass box as the site of an ontological rupture—it is the principal focus of the last three chapters.

How did the charming, small-town, and geographically-bounded world of Twin Peaks (population: 51,201) unravel into the vast and fragmented spatio-temporal expanse that confronts us in *The Return*? Sprawl is the theme of Richard Martin's contribution which, in addition to laying claim to being, alongside Todd McGowan's contribution, one of the first serious examinations of Michael Cera's celebrated cameo as Wally Brando, takes on the series' unmistakable depiction of "a world escaping and exceeding its usual boundaries, spilling out in unexpected directions at uneven speeds". Revisiting its numerous scattered locations, Martin's perceptive reflection approaches the various kinds of sprawl of *The Return*, embracing the term's geographic, temporal, and psychological resonances and the sprawling, free-associative formal level of the series itself.

Like Agent Cooper's comeback in *Twin Peaks: The Return*, Todd McGowan's keynote address was the most anticipated paper of the conference (albeit without the earth-shattering destitution that the eventual return of everyone's favourite FBI man brought in its wake), combining a sustained and compelling reading of *The Return* with the opportunity to revisit and reflect on many of the series' most beloved characters and moments. Noticing, as Martin does, that much of the narrative of *The Return* takes us away from the idyllic small-town setting of Twin Peaks, McGowan interrogates the distance that separates *The Return* from the original series in terms of the fantasmatic underpinnings of the *Twin Peaks* universe and its inherent impasse. Focusing extensively on the long-awaited revival of Agent Cooper in the season's closing episodes, McGowan traces the logic of fantasy which, rather than restoring the previous state of affairs for which viewers were so nostalgic, pushes instead to an encounter with its own internal limit point: the traumatic loss around which the first two seasons were largely constructed. In McGowan's reading, the closing episodes of *The Return* present something of a cautionary tale: in striving to avert Laura Palmer's murder before it has happened, Cooper's efforts amount to an attempt to eliminate the traumatic loss that founds subjectivity itself, effectively redoubling the traumatic violence through which the subject comes into being.

What happened to Audrey? What does Lynch reflect about America today? Who is the dreamer? The closing chapter of this volume is an edited transcript of the panel discussion on *Twin Peaks: The Return* that made up the final session of the Freud/Lynch conference. In addition to Richard Martin, Allister Mactaggart, and Todd McGowan, all of whom had discussed *The Return* in their respective papers, the panel also included psychoanalyst Tamara Dellutri, to whom we had assigned the task of watching *The Return* in the space of a week, without having seen the previous seasons or *Fire Walk With Me*. While deciphering is surely one of the great pleasures of Lynch spectatorship, we were interested to see what kinds of readings of *The Return* could emerge in the absence of any in-depth contextual knowledge of the *Twin Peaks* universe—readings which, without having recourse to the series' mythology, might be less encumbered by the task of attempting to resolve the series into some final all-encompassing explanation, and freer to orient themselves by the points of inconsistency and rupture of which explanatory readings are typically intolerant. The discussion opens with Dellutri's response to *The Return* before opening out into a wide-ranging conversation touching on themes of communication, technology, capitalism, repetition, nostalgia, and sincerity, revisiting along the way some of the season's defining moments.

Coda

It should be clear by now that our subtitle involves a sleight of hand. Far from implying that behind appearances lies a hidden reality—and tempting as such a proposition may be when we recall the traumatic revelations of *Twin Peaks: Fire Walk With Me* or the covertly witnessed scenes in Dorothy's apartment in *Blue Velvet*—the promise of disclosing a concealed reality behind appearances can only ever be a false one. Lynch's trademark red curtains have more in common with the famous anecdote from antiquity of the painting contest between Zeuxis and Parrhasius: when the time comes to reveal their paintings, Zeuxis unveils a painting so realistic that birds fly down to peck at the canvas. Trying to pull back the curtain to reveal his rival Parrhasius's entry, he is taken aback to find that he himself has been duped: what Parrhasius has painted is the curtain itself! The story, enthusiastically alluded to by Lacan in his eleventh seminar (1977, p. 103), is an apt reminder that although there is nothing behind it, the curtain engages each of us as spectators with the traces of our own peculiar nothing: a nothing which enables us to find and lose ourselves in Lynch's films, just as we do in the analytic transference. "The foundation of such a method", as *Twin Peaks*' Albert Rosenfeld (Miguel Ferrer) puts it, "is love".

References

Freud, S. (1900a). *The Interpretation of Dreams. S. E.*, 4–5. London: Hogarth.

Freud, S. (1901b). *The Psychopathology of Everyday Life. S. E.*, 6. London: Hogarth.

Freud, S. (1919h). The "Uncanny". *S. E.*, 17. London: Hogarth.

Freud, S. (1928b). Dostoevsky and Parricide. *S. E.*, 21. London: Hogarth.

Freud, S. (1930a). *Civilization and its Discontents. S. E.*, 21. London: Hogarth.

Frost, M. (2016). *The Secret History of Twin Peaks.* London: Macmillan.

Lacan, J. (1977). *The Four Fundamental Concepts of Psycho-Analysis.* London: Hogarth.

Lacan, J. (1991). *The Seminar of Jacques Lacan. Book II: The Ego in Freud's Theory and in the Technique of Psychoanalysis 1954–1955.* New York, NY: Norton.

Lynch, D. (2007). *Catching the Big Fish: Meditation, Consciousness, and Creativity.* New York, NY: TarcherPerigee—Penguin Random House.

Lynch, D. & Holdengräber, P. (2014). David Lynch in Conversation. Interview. Brooklyn Academy of Music, 29 April.

Masson, J. M. (1985). *The Assault on Truth: Freud's Suppression of the Seduction Theory.* Reading: Penguin.

Rodley, C. (Ed.) (2005). *Lynch on Lynch (Revised Edition).* New York, NY: Farrar, Straus, and Giroux.

CHAPTER 1

"Listen, do you want to know a secret?" Lynch stays silent

Chris Rodley

Since the shock appearance of his first feature-length movie *Eraserhead* in 1977, David Lynch has continued to produce work that often seems to come out of nowhere. Intensely personal, it is challenging not only in its visual aesthetic and complex use of sound, but also in its approach to storytelling. However, it's important to acknowledge that his highly individual and instantly recognisable work—work that is so specific it has become an adjective ("Lynchian")—does not exist in a vacuum; that it is part of the flow of cinema history and how we think and talk about the moving image at any one time; what we have come to expect of cinema, and of those who make it.

That said, Lynch's work does seem increasingly aberrant, primarily in its absolute determination to dream, and it's here that the Lynch/ Freud relationship really sparks. Lynch seems to be virtually alone these days in seeing both cinema and television as perfect places in which to dream. His characters frequently talk about their dreams, and those very dreams often hijack the screen unannounced. However, Lynch's entire practice is, in itself, a dreaming process. I would argue that this, in part, explains his almost legendary unwillingness—or inability—to "explain" what he releases into the world.

In recent years we've all witnessed the onslaught of "reality television" and its dominance in the schedules. However, with the notable exception of *Twin Peaks: The Return* (2017), no one seems to be making "dream television". Perhaps we're not even sure what that might look like these days. As a consequence, we're certainly not that well equipped to either recognise that it's happening or to understand it easily when it does.

You won't find much dreaming in contemporary cinema either, although you will find an increasing interest in, and reliance on, narratives involving alternative realities (Christopher Nolan's *Inception* (2010) being a prime example of this) or pure fantasy (*Game of Thrones* (2011–2019), etc.). At the other end of the scale, you will also find a lot of depictions of "real-life" situations, or movies that announce themselves as being "inspired by" or "based on" actual events. These are sometimes presented in such a visceral way that any abstractions are lost in their frantic pacing and in-your-face shooting and editing styles, in their determination to produce an immersive effect by grabbing the viewer by the throat. By beating the viewer into submission. So whilst Kathryn Bigelow rightfully deserved a long-overdue Best Director Oscar for her movie *The Hurt Locker* (2008), her lesser-known film, *Blue Steel* (1989), made twenty years previously, is far more interesting from the perspectives of psychoanalysis, phantasy, and internal states of mind.

Gone (apparently) are the days of movies such as John Boorman's *Point Blank* (1967). Masquerading as a West Coast gangster revenge story, the film is pure dream material. The main character Walker (the clue is in the name), played by Lee Marvin, is either dreaming the entire movie at the point of dying or he's a ghost. Or maybe it's all just a memory of some kind. Or maybe—just like Betty Elms/Diane Selwyn in Lynch's *Mulholland Drive* (2001) or Fred Madison in *Lost Highway* (1997)—he's just trying to imagine a better outcome for himself in the face of defeat, desperation, and death. Whatever the answer, it's a film gripped by the uncanny, but played out in the harsh, all-seeing sunlight of LA, not in the shadows.

As mainstream Hollywood movies—most of them produced in the town in which Lynch has lived for decades—have abdicated from so many areas of interest, newer, more independent studio-style operations and sensibilities have rushed in to fill the void in terms of subject matter. However, truly radical alternative aesthetics or approaches to storytelling haven't been a conspicuous outcome of this territorial grab. Lynch, on the other hand, has become increasingly uncompromising over the years.

Just as his work has become more challenging to decode, his reluctance to talk about it has inevitably increased; the more it screams out for explanations, the more audiences want to know. "What is it about?" might be a question that most directors could negotiate, but "What does it *mean*?" is surely the one question that they most dread. With Lynch, you are often forced to ask an additional question: "What is actually happening"?

This is one reason why the dream dimension of Lynch's work is a major factor in his silence. In Lynch's universe, dreaming isn't merely something you do when you're asleep—it can also be something triggered by hope, desire, or, more often than not, by kinds of aspiration or desperation. It becomes imagining a different life for yourself, often in response to bad actions you've committed in your regular existence. Perhaps, when long-lost Federal Agent Phillip Jeffries (David Bowie) appears (and doesn't appear) in *Twin Peaks: Fire Walk With Me* (1992), and says "we live inside a dream", this is what he means; that the lives we create for ourselves are comprised of alternative realities, outcomes, and even different versions of ourselves. We repurpose events, objects, and people from our day-to-day lives in order to create other, more interesting or happier lives for ourselves.

Talking about that kind of existence is difficult to describe. When you wake from having a disturbing dream and you try to explain it to another person, you realise in the process of explaining it that it is impossible to describe in words the one thing that most terrified you. That's because it was a mood, or a feeling. You might be describing in detail what actually happened, and reliving the dread as you do so, but you can see from the listener's face that it isn't scary to them. It really is a case of "you had to be there". Words become hopelessly inadequate or redundant. What Lynch does is make us experience the uncertainty, the unease, and the dread.

We need to look no further than a much-discussed scene in episode fourteen of *Twin Peaks: The Return* to discover something essential about Lynch's dream project. Gordon Cole (played by Lynch himself) describes a dream that he's had about meeting Italian actress Monica Bellucci in

Paris. Over a coffee (of course), Bellucci intones: "We are like the dreamer who dreams and then lives inside the dream". Here the camera dwells on close-ups of Gordon Cole's reactions in the dream, and close-ups of him telling us about the dream we're watching. Then Bellucci says, "But who is the dreamer?" Cole then tells us that in the dream he was suddenly overcome by a powerful, uneasy feeling. We can see Cole/Lynch both thinking about and remembering the dream. Bellucci looks past him, indicating that he should turn around. When he does, Cole sees himself as a younger man. Lynch sees the same thing, but he's looking at himself acting Gordon Cole in the feature film *Twin Peaks: Fire Walk With Me* from 1992. To me, the answer to the question "Who is the dreamer?" is that it's David Lynch himself. That's why he doesn't like to talk about it. What really matters in his dream would elude his words.

We all live inside a dream of sorts—inside our own mishmash of fantasies, hopes, disappointments, desires, and aspirations. As we are all dreamers in that sense, Lynch doesn't need to talk about the specifics of his own; we will do the talking for him because we do have a sense of what these images and events might mean to us. The internet is clogged with analyses of, for instance, the world of Twin Peaks. Much of this discussion is extremely complex. Some fans have made sophisticated videos, or created highly edited montages of images taken from the series, to help visualise their own theories. Lynch knows that he's turning audiences into active, thinking participants, some of whom he's also turning into filmmakers in the process. He knows that we might all see the exact same things, but that we will all come to different conclusions—ones that work for us in our own lives. He knows that if he ever said "this means this", that it will only ever mean that, and nothing else, forever. What it means to him is his business. What it means to us is all that matters. This brings us to the issue of intentionality.

I come from a generation that was heavily influenced by the "auteur theory". First proposed in the 1940s by the French critic André Bazin and then refined under the banner "*La politique des auteurs*" by François Truffaut in the 1950s, this is an ultimately reductive concept that claims the director has a kind of pure autonomy over his films (I say "he" because the director seemed always to be a man in those days). Even with all the complexities of the old Hollywood studio system, in which the director might have to please studio bosses, scriptwriters, producers, and sometimes even the stars, auteur theory was the idea that a good director would manage to stamp his concerns and aesthetics on every film he made. In the 1960s, courtesy of American film critic Andrew Sarris, this approach became even more extreme under the user-friendly name of the "auteur theory". In his book *The American Cinema: Directors and Directions (1929–1968)*, he even produced league tables of directors, ranking them from "pantheon level", "second tier", and "third tier" directors (Sarris, 1968). Unsurprisingly, there were a mere five women out of 250 directors on the list.

In the 1970s, when psychoanalysis became a tool with which to understand the various operations of cinema, the notion of auteur theory became less important because we became less concerned with intentionality. Instead, we could take a film and put *it* on the couch, rather than expect its supposed true author, the director, to provide the answers. In John Ford's disturbed and disturbing western *The Searchers* (1956), starring John Wayne as Ethan Edwards, we could now view the Native American tribe that wreaks such havoc at the beginning of the film, triggering a five-year odyssey ending in virtual madness for Wayne's character, as a representation of his repressed desire for his brother's wife. The tribe may not actually exist. It's Ethan's desire for his sister-in-law that threatens the survival of the homestead.

Now it was not necessary for Ford to confirm or deny this. Now it was up to the viewer to decide what was really happening, for the viewer to "read" the film, not for the director to explain the text. It's highly likely that Ford knew nothing of what he might have been doing on one level, and wouldn't have had a clue how to respond if asked about this kind of thing, which is just as well. They might well have damaged their stock at the studios by sounding too smart, or talking about ideas that the cinema audience might have little or no knowledge of.

Unfortunately, intentionality has been making something of a comeback. Possibly in part as a consequence of the explosion of various media platforms on which to talk about and promote movies and television series, we now want the director to tell us what it's all about. We need confirmation. Again. Indeed, we have come to expect them to be able to do this as part of their job. So too do the companies who make the films, as well as publicists, the press, and everyone else involved in the releasing or streaming of a movie these days. We expect directors to be articulate.

To Lynch's credit, he doesn't play this game. He wants to turn all of us into detectives, rather than be the narcissistic Hercule Poirot figure in the room, mixing all the clues together until they eventually become concrete—into just one, hard thing.

When I was writing *Lynch on Lynch* (1997) twenty years ago, I went to LA to work with David (I'm going to call him David for this bit). We recorded approximately fifty hours of talk over the course of a week or so, drank endless cups of coffee (of course), and—between us—smoked maybe fifty packs of cigarettes. It was difficult for both of us, but for entirely different reasons. I remember thinking, as it was happening, that much of the conversation felt either unenlightening or trivial. This was almost certainly due in part to the fact that I'd been reading Michel Chion's excellent book, *David Lynch* (1995), prior to the trip as part of my research. Interestingly, Chion is an experimental music composer—and one-time proponent of the *musique concrète* movement—as well as being a film theorist. Whilst lecturing at the Sorbonne in Paris, he had been looking at the relationship between image and sound, specifically in the cinema.

Every time I asked David a question arising from some of the theories in Chion's book, he just didn't respond. He was either unwilling or unable to engage with any specific reading of anything in his work. "I don't know, Chris" became the daily mantra. And yet every session was a glorious experience in some way or another. At one point, he almost convinced me that my cup of coffee might go cold due to me ignoring it whilst I was thinking or doing something else at the same time. It did always go cold on me. On another, his young son Riley began calling from outside the house, "Dad! I'm outside". And he was. For whatever reason, I never wanted to leave. Caffeine and nicotine poisoning, however, got the better of me.

Having thought about it a lot since, I realised that there are probably many reasons for Lynch's studied silence. It might begin with his mistrust of words and of language in general, because words limit meaning. It's also well documented that he has had a tortured relationship with words and that he has said on more than one occasion that talking can be dangerous.

However, it's very obvious that he likes the *sound* of words, phrases, and names, and this is evident in the way he speaks. He exaggerates particular words and you can often feel he struggles to verbalise certain concepts. In his short film *The Alphabet* (1968), you see a child literally terrorised by letters and words, which his then-wife Peggy Reavey described as a moment in his life where he was going through something comparable to a "pre-verbal stage", when he didn't say very much at all. And what about those single letters found under the fingernails of BOB's victims in *Twin Peaks*?

In order to produce a cinema that dreams, you have to keep tedious reality at bay. Part of the plot for *Lost Highway* is now attributed to one of the most infamous news stories of the time: the O. J. Simpson trial for the murder of his former wife, Nicole Brown Simpson, and her friend, Ron Coleman, in 1994. It was not until years later that Lynch admitted this, because he didn't want the reality of a real-life trial to limit the audience's response to the film. It certainly didn't figure in either his or co-writer Barry Gifford's imaginative spin on it: a complex depiction of how the mind of a two-time murderer might cope with the horrible reality of what he has done. Interestingly, the deeply mysterious, constantly surprising, and exhilarating depiction of a murderer's mind attempting to establish some kind of equilibrium that was the drama of *Lost Highway* turned out to be a recognised condition in the real world. And it had a name. They had stumbled on the "psychogenic fugue"—something else that Lynch studiously avoided mentioning when talking about the movie at the time. What helps to make *Lost Highway* a truly compelling experience is the fact that they didn't know about the condition first and then set out to write a movie about it—an illustration of it. They imagined a dramatic situation and, in following its own logic, parachuted us right inside the condition as a result.

Keeping certain facts behind his films a secret could be seen as a defence mechanism. Lynch exerts a high degree of control on all aspects of his work during its making. However, he knows that this ceases when it's released into the world. If it's being shown in cinemas, he cannot control whether it's loud enough or even if it's in focus at every location; if it's being streamed in people's homes, he cannot control whether the settings on their TVs are correct, or if they only have tinny speakers. He cannot control what audiences will make of it (he doesn't want to), what journalists critics will say about it, or what they'll ask him when he has to promote the work on press tours. It's painful for him that all of this is out of his control, and this most likely contributes to why he dislikes interviews so much—he has no control over them.

When *Lynch on Lynch* was finished, the galleys were sent to him in LA prior to its publication in 1997 so that he could agree the final text. This seemed only right, given that his words comprised a majority of the book—it was certainly not something he had insisted on. The publisher Faber and Faber always worked this way on their books about film directors, with the subject retaining copyright in their own words. My guess is that Lynch probably dreaded receiving those galleys, and dreaded even more having to then read them.

I presume he did, because he called me and said, "Chris, we should call this book *Horseshit on Horseshit*! Did I really say those things?" He had, of course. It was a playful call, but we did end up cutting a few pages of text. Much of this was about Transcendental Meditation and how it related to his work. So something has changed in the last twenty years. These days Lynch can and will talk at length and in great detail about the benefits of Transcendental Meditation and how it can unleash the creativity that is in us all.

However, as for the work itself and what it might mean, we'll have to keep looking for ourselves. Clues are everywhere, you just have to recognise the important ones. Sometimes they are in plain sight. In a recent interview, he said goodbye to the interviewer by saying, "Stay out of trouble, Gaby". It's a throwaway line, but it seems to resonate. Trouble is always just around the corner, and to avoid it is difficult. You have to be constantly vigilant, in part because trouble is fascinating. Trouble can be tempting. As David Lynch shows us in *Twin Peaks: The Return*, evil is inevitable, but good is steadfast.

References

Chion, M. (1995). *David Lynch*. London: British Film Institute.

Rodley, C. (1997). *Lynch on Lynch*. London: Faber & Faber.

Sarris, A. (1968). *The American Cinema: Directors and Directions (1929–1968)*. New York, NY: Dutton.

CHAPTER 2

What's so Lynchian about that? Defining a cultural moment with some notes from Freud and Lacan

Carol Owens

We live in a time when it is possible to say that something is or is not "Lynchian". To be able to describe a cultural moment or time in the terms of a signifier which is also a name is to confer upon that signifier the status of what Lacan calls a master signifier (Lacan, 2007, pp. 37–38). It is a master signifier since it gathers together the elements, characteristics, and traits that constitute a discourse as an epistemic operation, with an identifiable *technē* or crafted set of practices. However, it is my argument in this essay that for there to be a "Lynchian", there already had to be "the Freudian", understood again as epistemic. In this sense, "the Lynchian" is a type of palimpsest, relying as it does on the underwriting of what is constituted as "the Freudian". As a Freudo-Lacanian psychoanalyst, I see and hear the operation of the Lynchian palimpsest in the various formations and products of the unconscious going on in his work; the cadence of the joke, the disturbance of the dream, the play of the symptom. My approach will be to examine some of these unconscious formations in Lynch's work, showing how they are thoroughly Freudian, and to trace some of the lines along which they are knotted together with cultural products and commentary.

David Lynch has made clear at various moments in interviews on his work that he is not attempting to do something psychoanalytic; sometimes he mentions "the sub-conscious" (Lynch & Rodley, 2005, p. 64), more rarely Freud, whereas he's quite happy to speak about "consciousness" and in particular its transcendence (Lynch, 2006). Against a facile "Freudian" take on his work—the notion of a "hidden meaning" or interpretation—he's keen to respond that he hasn't overly thought about injecting meaning, hidden or otherwise, into his work (Lynch & Rodley, 2005). Upping the ante even, he claims that he either doesn't know what he is doing, or that what he is doing isn't always convertible into words (ibid.). To be clear, David Lynch doesn't need to be a Freudian in order for the cultural moment that is "the Lynchian" to be so.

Even worse than the real thing—the Lynchian joke is on you!

Let's begin with a scene from episode eight of the Netflix TV show *Girlboss* (2017), based on the rags-to-riches story of Sophia Amoruso and her online vintage shop Nasty Gal. We join "Nasty Gal" in a moment of tension on an internet forum where her vintage-selling competitors are not happy with her trading practices. First, there is an assertion by Nasty Gal that the message board should be called "David Lynch's *Elephant Man*" because it's "full of freaks and sad as fuck" (my preferred title for this essay, incidentally). Then there is the received insult articulated by one of the forum members: "she called us freaks". Finally, there is the delivery of what I am calling the Freudian/Lynchian punch-line from another forum member: "*Even worse*, she completely missed the point of *The Elephant Man*".

The scene perfectly captures the paradoxical resonances of Lynch's work in mainstream culture. True, his films are apparently filled with freaks and sad fucks. However, and this is the most important part of this joke sequence—as well as being proof of the full-on cultural insertion of the work of David Lynch, it's possible to *miss the point* of David Lynch. If it is possible to miss the point of him, this is a way to say that there is a point to David Lynch and that it is something about which cultural commentaries and discourses may be in agreement.

So there are two really important and quite sophisticated things going on here. One is how David Lynch's work, and getting what David Lynch's films and work are about, is used in order to make fun of the internet forum; the other is that it's not even possible to make this joke, to make people smile or even laugh when this scene takes place, without the possibility of the viewing audience of the TV show to be able to "get the joke". In order for a joke, or what Freud (1905c) called the *Witz*, to be laughed at, a whole different kind of operation needs to take place at the location of what Lacan calls the big Other.

The scene from *Girlboss* may be regarded as having the structure of what Freud called a tendentious joke. An example from Woody Allen is almost identical in structure. Opening scene, *Annie Hall* (1977): two Jewish women are complaining about a holiday resort. One woman says the food in the resort is so bad, the other agrees and adds—even worse, the portion sizes are too small. Allen's own version as voice-over is "life is full of suffering but even worse it's over too soon". Like the dish in the restaurant, like life, David Lynch may give you something to complain about, but even worse, you may be left with your lack, with what is missing to you. In Freudian terms, one of the reasons why a joke such as this "even worse" formula makes us laugh is that it satisfies the conditions of the tendentious joke.

In his book *Jokes and their Relation to the Unconscious* (1905), Freud argues that a joke allows us to exploit something ridiculous in our enemy which we could not, on account of certain obstacles in the way, bring forward openly or consciously (Freud, 1905c, p. 103). The success of what he called "the tendentious joke" relies, however, upon the response of the Other to whom it is addressed in order for it to be ratified as a joke. Jacques Lacan begins his fifth seminar—*The Formations of the Unconscious* (2017)—with a vigorous investigation of the joke. What interests him about jokes is not so much the techniques and styles that Freud so carefully examines in his work, but rather, on the one hand, what it is that could be said to be contained in the joke as a message and, on the other, to whom this message is addressed. Lacan's use of the Freudian joke is mobilised in order to illuminate something important about the passage of the signifier and its subsequent reception in the big Other.

Lacan claims that the witticism or joke is the message conveyed to the Other in the form of a demand for it to be authenticated as such. If the joke succeeds in becoming authenticated, the subject receives the bounty of the pleasure, which for Lacan is akin to the same primitive pleasure he has received from his first use of the signifier, in the first use of demand addressed to a first big Other. That the big Other consents to, or resists, what is manifest in the message, is contingent upon the Other knowing what you are talking about; in other words, the appeal of the joke finds its mark in the Other because the message is concurrent with the code at that place. Lacan explains:

> Confirmation by the Other […] is essential here. The Other […] places the message in the code as a witticism, he says in the code, 'this is a witticism'. If no one does this, there is no witticism. (Lacan, 2017, p. 18)

Lacan here is referring to the big Other as the treasury of signifiers and all the metaphorical implications that from the beginning are piled up in language in a latent state in the interlocutor. This together with the archive of human images formed and conditioned via the interrelation of human beings enculturated in societies is what Lacan calls the signifying management of human economy. This is, in other words, the symbolic Other; the Other as locus of the symbolic order.

If it is possible to miss the point of David Lynch's *The Elephant Man* (1980)—or any other of his films—then this is a way to say that there is a place in the big Other which identifies, ratifies, and endorses the Lynchian message. This is the essential condition for the joke in *Girlboss* to arrive—like the Lacanian letter—at its destination; we laugh because the tendentious structure of the joke allows us to laugh at those who miss the point of David Lynch. Lol. But also, we laugh because behind that, or beneath that, maybe we have missed the point of David Lynch ourselves. It's not for nothing that so much digital and print material is dedicated to explaining the point of David Lynch's work, or in Todd McGowan's phrase, the point of its impossibility (McGowan, 2007, p. 25).

In dreams

Perhaps the most readily recognisable component of what constitutes "the Freudian", and therefore "the Lynchian", is the dream. Dreams, dreaming, dreamers, and nightmares (both waking and sleeping versions) are everywhere in Lynch's work. Dream sequences take on emblematic and iconic resonance as viewers ponder the meanings of dreams in specific films and in specific episodes of *Twin Peaks* (1990–1991). In what is touted as the "greatest dream scene in the history of television" (Rossi, 2017), the episode from *Twin Peaks* series one entitled "Zen, or the Skill to Attract a Killer" has attracted much academic attention as well as endless internet threads and commentaries from fans. According to "The Man from Another Place" (Michael J. Anderson) in this dream, the woman who resembles Laura Palmer is "filled with secrets".

The dream for Freud is also filled with secrets, containing as it does a "tangle of dream-thoughts which cannot be unravelled", what he refers to as the dream's "navel", or the "spot where it reaches into the unknown" (Freud, 1900a, p. 525). Here's a scene from a very bad dream:

> what he sees in there, these turbinate bones covered with a whitish membrane, is a horrendous sight [...] Everything blends in and becomes associated in this image, from the mouth to the female sexual organ, by way of the nose [...] There's a horrendous discovery here, that of the flesh one never sees, the foundation of things, the other side of the head, of the face, the secretory glands par excellence, the flesh from which everything exudes, at the very heart of the mystery, the flesh in as much as it is suffering, is formless, in as much as its form in itself is something which provokes anxiety. Spectre of anxiety, identification of anxiety, the final revelation of *you are this—you are this, which is so far from you, this which is the ultimate formlessness.*

It's not a scene you missed from one of Lynch's films, although it could be. Actually, it is Jacques Lacan describing a dream of Freud's, which he calls the "dream of dreams" (Lacan, 1991, pp. 154–155). According to Lacan, the meaning of the dream is revealed to Freud as "the nature of the symbolic" (ibid. p. 160). Freud referred to the site of the formation of the dream as *ein anderer Schauplatz*—another scene or stage—where something truly different takes place, an unconscious phenomenon on the symbolic level, decentred in relation to the ego (Freud, 1900a, p. 536). Lynch creates "The Man from Another Place", who acts as a spokesperson for the unconscious phenomenon in Cooper's (Kyle MacLachlan) experience: sphinx-like, he conveys the message to Cooper that Laura Palmer is a treasure trove of secret messages. For Freud, as for Lacan, what is successfully transmitted in the dream is a message, despite its having been distorted (a bit like the speech of "The Man from Another Place" and of Laura Palmer), ciphered, and so on. What's more, it isn't even important for us to understand its meaning. Indeed, while its interpretation may suggest a meaning that is unrecognisable or difficult for us to accept, it is enough to recognise that something is being transmitted in the form of a message, and that this has a sense, a meaning.

The function of dreams, as Lacan emphasises, is not to guard sleep but to pass a message (Lacan, 1991, p. 159). And this is so much a part of our symbolic order that in the most banal of exchanges there is the idea that a dream passes a message from the unconscious to the dreamer, which is interpretable by the dreamer and by the others to whom she explains her dream. In this way, in our time, the words "I had a dream last night" can be followed by the enquiry "what was it about?" This taken-for-granted aspect of dreaming as having meaning has a place in our symbolic order—and just like the joke's requirement to be understood in that same place, so too the very idea that dreams have meaning particular to the dreamer is the Freudian discovery. His dream of dreams revealed to him that he was haunted by the fear that he would be disgraced by being found to be incompetent.

Lynch's dreams make use of this fundamental Freudian discovery: that the dream reveals to the dreamer what he already knows but has made a secret of to him/herself. This is clear even in the scene from *Blue Velvet* (1986) where Sandy (Laura Dern) tells Jeffrey (Kyle MacLachlan) her "robins" dream. There is the dream narrative and there is Sandy's interpretation since the dream narrative is coded, enciphered as it were, by her, for her ("I guess it means there is trouble until the robins come"). The Lynchian dream message can—like the joke's punch-line—only hit its mark if as speaking beings we are familiar with, and receptive to, the unconscious, and its formations and products, and find in them meaning and signification.

That a dream is interpretable, or decipherable, also means that it is open to interpretation, and we share then in the suspicion around certain dream interpretations, which are not commensurate with our own theories about dream-work. This little twist is brilliantly exposed later in that same episode of *Twin Peaks*, in what is surely one of the most comical scenes from the show. Cooper, keen to share the insights from his dream—the fomenting of a method to catch a killer—engages Sheriff Truman (Harry Ontkean), Deputies Hawk (Michael Horse) and Andy (Harry Goaz), and Lucy (Kimmy Robertson) in a pantomime of calling out all the names of the people Laura Palmer was associated with containing the letter "J", then aiming a rock at a glass bottle and depending on whether the bottle is struck, the name is judged to be of some or no significance. Some three minutes into this demonstration, Sheriff Truman pulls Cooper to one side and asks: "So, Coop. Tell me … the idea for this really came from a dream?" "Yes, it did". Cooper replies. Both question and answer are delivered deadpan. Here, Lynch has a laugh at Freud. "So, Freud. Tell me … the idea for the unconscious really came from a dream?" "Yes, it did". However, it is also an opportunity to subvert the attempts of viewers to pin a specific meaning to Cooper's dream; thereby highlighting how much we cleave on the one hand to the potential of the dream to reveal its secrets, but also, then, how much we are left with the dream's point of nonsense—its navel, as Freud described it.

And indeed it is the very point of apparent nonsense—often obscene—in a dream that constitutes for many people a Lynchian moment. But it works in reverse too; in other words, the nonsensical, disturbing moments of waking life can appear dreamlike as they touch the real kernel or navel of unconscious desire. A client of mine described an incident after she had taken her ageing mother, who had had a stroke, to live with her in her home. She had attempted to touch up her mother's hair colour but did not manage to get the correct hair dye. As she works on her mother's head, the dye reveals a dramatic blood-red hue, and as the client is unaccustomed to handling the product, it ends up on the floor, the mother's head, and parts of her face and throat. Quite a lot of things in the room are all now vividly red. At that very minute, the social worker, who had planned a later visit to check in on the mother following her hospital stay, arrives unexpectedly at the house ahead of schedule. The client remarks: "I swear to God it was like a dream out of a David Lynch film, I must have looked like I was murdering my mother!" Naturally, it doesn't bear asking in this case "which film?" Notwithstanding the maternal ambivalence *mise-en-scène* in the look-alike murder and the signifiers of blood and dye (die), it is through what is seen by the social worker, whose gaze functions as David Lynch's camera, that the scene resembles a dream, and a Lynchian one at that. In what is essentially a collapsing of fantasy (unworked-through ambivalence about the sick and ageing mother) and unconscious desire (mother murdered/dying), the twin elements—fantasy/desire—that Lynch deploys juxtaposed throughout his work are assembled together in the client's experience, and the client finds herself, on (the Lynchian) stage as it were, in the act of killing.

There is another essentially Freudian formulation of dream-work worthy of mention going on in Lynch. What happens when the dream switches from one narrative form to another, when there is a change of scene, or when there is a dream within a dream? When is the right moment to wake up, and who are we in those moments if, as Lacan puts it, the ego is out of play? Looking back on Freud's dream of dreams—the dream of Irma's injection—Lacan claims that when Freud looked down Irma's throat he was faced with what he calls "the real lacking any possible mediation, the ultimate real, of the essential object which isn't an object any longer, but the object of anxiety par excellence", and at that moment Freud as ego disappears in the dream (Lacan, 1991, pp. 154–155). There's no Freud any longer, he says, no longer anyone who can say "I". Lacan's idea is that what is at stake in the function of the dream is beyond the ego—that is to say, what in the subject is of the subject and not of the subject, the unconscious (ibid. p. 159). As such, when the ego disappears in a dream as he claims Freud's ego does in his dream of Irma's injection it is because it is distributed across a range (three ranges, in fact) of imaginary identifications. This helps Lacan to understand why Freud doesn't wake up at the point in the dream where we might expect him to (ibid. p. 155). This brilliant observation—of the dreamer's ego AWOL in the dream and of the expectation that upon awakening the ego is restored—is mobilised in the scene from *Mulholland Drive* where "Rita" (Laura Harring) wakes up. She says "I thought when I woke up sleep would do it [...] I don't know who I am [...] I don't know what my name is". But, since Rita is never really Rita, and waking up confers not a return to waking reality but rather a switch in narrative, Lynch distributes his protagonists' egos across a range of imaginary counterparts such that not only we, but they, are not always sure who are they are, nor whether they are still sleeping.

And to make matters worse they/we can't always wake up when they/we want to. The Cowboy's (Monty Montgomery) intervention "Hey pretty girl, time to wake up!" fails to work as an injunction. In his book *The Interpretation of Dreams* (1900), Freud tells the following dream recounted to him by a female patient:

> A father had been watching day and night beside the sick-bed of his child. After the child died, he retired to rest in an adjoining room, but left the door ajar so that he could look from his room into the next, where the child's body lay surrounded by tall candles. An old man, who had been installed as a watcher, sat beside the body, murmuring prayers. After sleeping for a few hours the father dreamed that the child was standing by his bed, clasping his arm and crying reproachfully: "Father, don't you see that I am burning?" The father woke up and noticed a bright light coming from the adjoining room. Rushing in, he found that the old man had fallen asleep, and the sheets and one arm of the beloved body were burnt by a fallen candle.
>
> (Freud, 1900a, p. 509)

About this dream, Lacan (1977) claims that what wakes the man up is another reality in the dream, which is more unbearable than the one he has fled from into sleep. And this other reality consists of the terrible vision of the dead child designating a beyond—which is not representable, but that makes itself heard in the dream. What is the dreamer in this absence of representability properly speaking? Here, we can grasp the whole ambiguity of the function of awakening and of the function of the real in this awakening. The real may be represented by the noise, the light, some small element of reality, something that gives us the heads up that we are not dreaming, and yet what actually wakes us up is the other reality hidden behind a lack of representability; what Lacan refers to as the unscreened real. And this is what we grasp when, in its various depictions, we encounter it in its Lynchian representations. At a moment when the dreamer could wake up, there is a disappearance, which we understand as a switch, at the point of the failure of representability. *Mulholland Drive* (2001) is a masterclass in this phenomenon of dreams.

In Freud's dream of Irma's injection and in the dream of the burning child, there is a traumatic encounter (the sight of Irma's throat, the vision of the burning son); in the second dream, the dreamer wakes up at this point, while in the first, the horror gives way to the arrival of Freud's doctor colleague/friends. The father's awakening from the second dream has the same function as the sudden change of tone in the first, insofar as it can be said that his reality enables him to evade an encounter with true trauma (Žižek, 2001). This bit of dream-work finds its way into many Lynchian film moments; in the clinic, clients describe these dream episodes and their waking reality counterparts as Lynchian dreams or daydreams, or even as Lynchian fever dreams. In a sense, we are constantly waiting for someone to finally wake up, so that we can get our bearings. Žižek attributes to Adorno the idea that the Nazi motto "*Deutschland, erwache!*" actually meant its opposite: "the promise that if you obey this call, you could continue to sleep and dream (i.e. to avoid engagement with the real of social antagonism)" (Žižek, 2002, p. 196). He elaborates this idea recalling that in the first stanza of Primo Levi's poem *Reveille* the concentration camp survivor remembers being in the camp, asleep dreaming intense dreams about returning home, eating, telling his relatives his story, when, suddenly, he is woken up by the Polish kapo's command *Wstawać!* (Get up!). In the second stanza, he is at home after the war, well-fed, having told his story to his family, when, suddenly, the shout, *Wstawać!* irrupts in his mind. Žižek argues that the reversal of the relationship between dream and reality from the first stanza to the second is crucial. Their content is formally the same—the pleasant domestic scene is interrupted by the injunction "get up!"—but in the first, the dream is cruelly interrupted by the wake-up call, while in the second, reality is interrupted by the imagined (or hallucinated) command (Žižek, 2002, p. 197).

The Lynchian symptom (like something out of David Lynch ...)

On the psychoanalyst's couch, the symptom is understood as representing a kind of question the client has about their individual relationship to their jouissance, and about their unconscious desire. On the other hand, we can think about the cultural symptom as a kind of index of the way a culture enjoys, and the way a culture suffers; even the way a culture desires, evidenced in its passions. The three great commentators on the social bond, Marx, Freud, and Lacan, variously describe how the way in which a culture suffers and responds to that suffering is in turn caught up with an economy of desire and satisfaction. Todd McGowan's work on the enjoyment of lack, and capitalism and desire also points up the cultural and social symptom in this way. Taking our bearings from a culture's passions, what then can we recognise as contemporary cultural symptoms and what—to ask the question of this essay—is so Lynchian about them?

I'm going to start with this one. There is a passion in our time for the "real" and the "true". As post-postmodern subjects, we suffer from a certain jadedness with relativism. However, our neoliberal-inflected understandings of what opposes relativism has us reach out to something which allows for different understandings of a phenomenon with shared epistemological status, and, at the same time, towards something that functions as an exception—working hard to get to a place of real, and true. It's the paradoxical desire of contemporary culture: I want to be everywhere at the same time, but also "be me" and be true. This "anything goes", but "only you can find what is true for you" is what so many readings of Lynch's work offer. The fabulous Naomi Watts describes working with David Lynch on *Mulholland Drive* in these terms. In the interview both Lynch and Watts are discussing Watts' casting for the film and the signifier *Mulholland Drive*. For Lynch, *Mulholland Drive* is

> a famous road (in LA) ... There is much much much mood—there's so many stories about that road and um, it's a really kind of dreamy thing to think about. You know the old stories—so many people come here to realise their dreams.

Then Watts:

> Mulholland Drive was a particular road that I would remember when I was down down down on my luck and I remember thinking: ooof, this day is going too bad and this has been a succession of really bad days and I could really [*mimes holding the steering wheel of a car*] just do a [*mimes jerking wheel suddenly to the left*] quick quick turn and just drive off this cliff ... [*laughs*] ... um ... no ... so ... but ... there are times when you just drive smoothly around and the light's right and it's the opposite of that and you know ... you're

> listening to the right song and so again I think it's a great symbolic thing that can mean a lot of great things to some people and a lot of very dark things. The long unending windy road.

Lynch's approach to take the iconic road rich with stories and mood for the setting of the film is laid out for us. Watts, however, indicates the subjective tension and torsion in her own drive along Mulholland Drive (from suicidal impulse to contented flow), which is quite at odds with Lynch's own description and yet entirely consonant with the cultural framing of ambivalent states of being; nowadays, "some people" are as likely to drive off the cliff as to enjoy the drive. But furthermore, the advantage of the symbolism of the road means (for Watts) that,

> We don't all have to have the same understanding; different things appeal to different people at different times and it's not all logical and making perfect sense but if it's real and true it links up and you can connect.

So the symbol, or we could say the signifier, "Mulholland Drive", functions to capture this everything and anything of the range of people's experiences in Los Angeles, but at the same time, and because it captures so much, it allows for a localising of the individual's connection with what is real and true. Or perhaps because a signifier takes on this kind of domestic function (to orientate the subject to what is a contemporary cultural experience or symptom—everything goes, everything has meaning—etc.), we need to join up the dots ourselves and decide that there is something real and true in it, since, otherwise, we "can't connect with it" in its illogicality and imperfect sense-making. It's a little bit like the Emperor's new clothes, is it not? We agree that he's wearing something even though we know he isn't, because no one wants to say otherwise; the calling out of something false is unpalatable to neoliberal taste; but the disavowal associated with the perverse desire to oscillate between forms or frames of meaning on the one hand, and the consequent yet paradoxical search for truth and connection on the other is what is salient in the contemporary cultural symptom and its jouissance.

Another passion of our times is for the bizarre. Guaranteed, the most often cited adjectives about Lynch's films are "strange", "weird", and "freaky". But why am I calling this a symptom, and why is it specifically Lynchian? Again, for a symptom to be shared via the signifier, just like the joke's punch-line, and the idea that dreams are full of meaning, or full of nonsense where the dreamer can be exposed to the most traumatic real, the symptom must also be registered with the big Other. In our time, there is nothing scarier than normalcy. In an interview between Patti Smith and David Lynch for BBC Arts, Smith invites Lynch to comment on the use of the song "Blue Velvet" by Bobby Vinton and the images Lynch uses in the film. Smith explains how when the song first came out,

> it repelled me and yet I was drawn to it and then seeing your film I re-accessed that weird uncomfortable trepidation I used to hear hearing that song. It's the illusion of something comforting or normal and what's more horrifying than normalcy really?

What's more horrifying than normalcy? Todd McGowan makes the point that Lynch's films seem bizarre to us precisely because of the excessiveness of their normality. Lynch is, in McGowan's words, "bizarrely normal" (McGowan, 2007, pp. 12–13). But through the act of taking normality to its logical extreme, Lynch reveals how the bizarre is not opposed to the normal but inherently within it. It is in this way that I understand what clients attempt to capture when they describe the "weirdly unweird", or the "oddly normal" as being "like something out of David Lynch". Like this scene where a client describes locking an over-excited young dog out in the garden while her disapproving mother-in-law comes to visit and, looking out through the window, sees the dog bouncing towards the French windows with a hammer between his teeth. The overdetermination of normalcy and its slide into the bizarre is played with to lesser or greater extent throughout much of Lynch's work. The opening scene of *Blue Velvet* is the classic example of this slide. Following Lynch's gaze beyond the lawn, and between the blades of grass, we end up alongside the camera surrounded by bugs. But this reference to a strangeness at the heart of being revealed in the suggestion of the uncanny relies upon another essential Freudian discovery; the *Unheimliche*, or uncanny, as that extimate point of our subjectivity. Lacan formulated the concept of "extimacy" in order to account for the point that is most intimate in the subject as inextricably linked with the Other (1992, p. 139). In other words, the Other is inside the subject occupying the place of extimacy. His famous formulation that man's desire is the Other's desire is an early indication of extimacy. But what is in fact extimate is most often experienced as a hateful revulsion of the Other, and moreover, of the Other's way of enjoying. It is this very jouissance, as the (hated) lack in the Other, which is in fact central to xenophobia. Indeed, since the alterity of the Other cannot be grounded in one signifier, hate, conditioned by the unbearable extimacy of the jouissance of the Other, is frequently grounded in the signifier of the animal invader; the most common human displacement of what is alien and undesirable, albeit fascinating and ultimately phobogenic (Swales & Owens, 2020, pp. 102–119). What, then, is deeply disturbing about the Other's jouissance—or at least, the subject's fantasy of it—results in an attempt to impose one's own supposedly superior mode of jouissance on the other, who is dehumanised in various ways. *Lost Highway* (1997) is exemplary in the demonstration of a monstrous "extimate" jouissance at play; the "Mystery Man" (Robert Blake) is the name of Fred's extimacy, the uncanny, repulsive unconscious enjoyment at the core of his psyche.

Dark Mofo Nude Solstice Swim, 2018, photo credit: Dark Mofo/Rémi Chauvin, courtesy of Dark Mofo, Hobart, Tasmania, Australia

The ultimate proof, however, that we live in "Lynchian" times is its commodification. The appetite for the bizarre, as the culturally acceptable expression of the relationship we have with our own extimate enjoyment, is now packaged as a Lynchian commodity. To my absolute delight, by pure chance, I came across some publicity material for a festival in Tasmania held in June 2018, which promoted the event as the kind of thing David Lynch would do if he did festivals, as the "darkest, weirdest, edgiest shit" could be found there. I got in touch with the people at Dark Lab who organise Dark Mofo—a midwinter festival celebrating the dark, through large-scale public art, music, feasting, light, sound, and noise across Hobert, Tasmania. The organisers say that Dark Mofo combines ancient traditions with contemporary ritualism to promote strange dreams and restless visions. They kindly shared with me a number of wonderful images from their June 2019 festival, which included scenes and sets straight from *Twin Peaks*; among other things, people could hang out at the Bang Bang Bar, congregate in front of shrines to Laura Palmer, hear Chrysta Bell and Rebekah Del Rio sing in concert, and for a final surreal act, they could participate in the annual summer solstice nude swim.

References

Freud, S. (1900a). *The Interpretation of Dreams. S.E.*, 4. London: Hogarth.

Freud, S. (1905c). *Jokes and their Relation to the Unconscious. S.E.*, 8. London: Hogarth.

Lacan, J. (1977). *The Four Fundamental Concepts of Psycho-Analysis*. London: Hogarth.

Lacan, J. (1991). *The Seminar of Jacques Lacan. Book II. The Ego in Freud's Theory and in the Technique of Psychoanalysis 1954–1955*. J.-A. Miller (Ed.). S. Tomaselli (Trans.). London: Norton & Co.

Lacan, J. (1992). *The Seminar of Jacques Lacan. Book VII. The Ethics of Psychoanalysis 1959–1960*. J.-A. Miller (Ed.). D. Porter (Trans.). London: Routledge.

Lacan, J. (2007). *The Seminar of Jacques Lacan. Book XVII. The Other Side of Psychoanalysis 1969–1970*. J.-A. Miller (Ed.). R. Grigg (Trans.). London: Norton.

Lacan, J. (2017). *The Seminar of Jacques Lacan. Book V. Formations of the Unconscious 1957–1958*. J.-A. Miller (Ed.). R. Grigg (Trans.). London: Polity Press.

Lynch, D. (2006). *Catching the Big Fish. Meditation, Consciousness, and Creativity*. New York, NY: Penguin Group.

Lynch, D. & Rodley, C. (Ed.) (2005). *Lynch on Lynch*. London: Faber & Faber.

McGowan, T. (2007). *The Impossible David Lynch*. New York: Columbia University Press.

Rossi, R. (2017). "Twin Peaks": We Analyzed TV's Greatest Dream Sequence. *The Wrap*. <https://www.thewrap.com/twin-peaks-dream-sequence-analysis-analyzed-dale-cooper-laura-palmer/> (last accessed 10 June 2020).

Swales, S. & Owens, C. (2020). *Psychoanalysing Ambivalence with Freud and Lacan: On and Off the Couch*. London: Routledge.

Žižek, S. (2001). *Enjoy Your Symptom! Jacques Lacan in Hollywood and Out*. London: Routledge.

Žižek, S. (2002). *Did Somebody Say Totalitarianism? Five Interventions in the (Mis)Use of a Notion*. London: Verso.

CHAPTER 3

Dream logic in *Mulholland Drive*

Olga Cox Cameron

Ever since I was, as *Finnegans Wake* (1939) would put it, "jung and easily freudened", I have been fascinated by the grammar, logic, and rhetoric of dreams explored by Freud. So of course I *would* see *Mulholland Drive* (2001) in this light. Reading it as a dream is a widely accepted approach, justifiable structurally and also narratively by the sound of someone sleeping under a green coverlet in the opening sequence and the injunction "Wake up, little girl", which closes the first fractured section of the film.

But can one say that it is justified formally? Dreams are a common enough representational trope despite being notoriously difficult to actually replicate in art forms. Good attempts which nonetheless fall short would be Akira Kurosawa's 1990 film *Dreams*, and Toby's dream in Janet Frame's 1957 novel *Owls Do Cry*. The one outstanding exception to falling short prior to *Mulholland Drive* is of course *Finnegans Wake*, and a fair question to ask is: did it succeed as well as it did because Joyce had in fact, at least partially, read *The Interpretation of Dreams* (1900)?

Among many scattered allusions, the *Wake* speaks of dream "irmages", referencing Freud's famous dream of Irma's injection, so this is not altogether a wildcard assumption. Although we don't get any analogous hint in David Lynch's work, we can nonetheless find in the narrative warps, which mark the first section of *Mulholland Drive*, an impressive number of what Freud lists as the modalities by which the unconscious speaks.

In a way it is paradoxical that Freud was even able to draw up a concrete list respecting such an evanescent phenomenon, and that in accessing it both Joyce and Lynch were able to create a dream analogue, an imaginary fabric repeatedly punctured in locatable ways by the incursions of an intolerable knowing. As Freud found out, talking about the unconscious is like playing with quicksilver. Epistemology is brought to bear on that which by its very nature resists it, since unconscious activity engages with a very specific form of not knowing, and furthermore one that functions as a pulsation rather than as a steadily identifiable phenomenon. A knowing that is simultaneously a refusal to know; a refusal to know that nonetheless knows. Something like the unstable representational edge of a high-octane force field, since clearly what must not be known is by no means trivial. To know would be to be unable to go on being, would be to snap shut the liveable space we as subjects manage to inhabit. Not just *Mulholland Drive* but our own dreams offer us instances of how we defend against this danger.

We have all experienced those moments when we wake up in sudden fright right on the cusp of horror, often blanking the dreamt lead-in provoking this fright. Lacan's seminar on *The Ego in Freud's Theory and in the Technique of Analysis* includes a terrific riff on how this occurs over and over in Freud's own specimen dream, the dream of Irma, pointing out how Freud, a "tough customer" according to Lacan (1991, p. 155), manages not to wake up at these danger points, but finds ploys which allow him to go on dreaming. In *Mulholland Drive*, what we take to be Diane's (Naomi Watts) dream would suggest that Diane too is a tough customer, given the numerous times that the dream veers towards, and then abruptly away from, a too-explicit reference to what she cannot let herself know.

In this great film, Lynch straight off engages with three of the questions Freud grappled with in *The Interpretation of Dreams*:

- What drives the dream?
- What is the relation between trauma and fantasy?

- How and why do apparently random bits and pieces of memory surface, very often striated by strangeness?

Originally Freud focused on the dream as wish fulfilment. It wasn't until 1920 with *Beyond the Pleasure Principle* that he fully took on board the magnetising power of trauma. This magnetising force is visible in *Mulholland Drive* in the repeated drift towards, and the abrupt sheering away from, what one might call nevralgic spots: dangerous allusions to its hidden underlay. Freud already had some inkling of this in 1900 when he suggested that dreams are the guardians of sleep and not its disturbers, meaning that the dream narrative can generally hold at bay these jolting encounters with traumatic truth. It does this, however, less by way of avoidance than by way of insistence and allusion, so that paradoxically, the whole dream is stained with what must not appear. In the case of *Finnegans Wake*, the word "incest", indicating that which troubles the entire dream, never appears as such, but is written in the thousands of insects, the pervasive ubiquity of the ant and grasshopper, in all kinds of entomological allusions and even in the wonderfully Shakespearian tale of Formio and Cigalette.

So what are the signature ploys of the dream-work listed by Freud and replicated by Lynch in Diane's dream?

Condensation

In the first instance we have what Freud (1900a) called condensation or compression: a propensity to weld multiplicities together without hierarchising them. In *Mulholland Drive*, a number of stories are carried by the same narrative current. Lynch describes this film as a love story, but it is an annihilatory love story in which it is not unreasonable to ask: "who kills whom?" and "can one annihilation happen without the other?" The opening sequence references two killings. The viewer follows a nocturnal car journey suffused with the red and black which are Camilla's (Laura Harring) signature colours. In real life it was Diane in the car, a Diane hopelessly in thrall to Camilla, and it was precisely her helpless in-loveness that was about to be murdered by Camilla's sadism. Both killings are implicit in this scene and the alarmed, vulnerable one is now Camilla. She speaks the words uttered by Diane, "What are you doing? We don't stop here", and which ushered in the devastating barrage of humiliation undergone at the dinner party, while the presence of the gun references the revenge pact with the hired killer. Diane's vulnerable smile as she walks up the path with Camilla shows what is about to be killed in her, and with what careful cruelty. Alongside these two stories present in the opening sequence a third silently insists, the love story with Hollywood itself, the Hollywood dream, and all the girls who have died in thrall to it.

Another compressing or condensing ploy favoured by the dream-work to carry several currents at once is the use of what Freud calls "switch words". No prizes for seeing the leitmotif of the film, the phrase "This is the Girl", as such a switch word. This is the girl Diane wants killed, the girl she is totally in love with, the girl who stars where Diane doesn't, the girl Camilla betrays her with in a lingering kiss staged for her benefit. This phrase, uttered in actuality by Diane to the hired killer, is one of the nevralgic points in the dream, veering very close to its unbearable core, so compression alone will not be enough to permit it to appear. Four of the other ploys listed by Freud will be pressed into service: displacement/distortion, the dream within a dream, absurdity, and reversal.

I would like briefly to show how and where these ploys appear elsewhere in the dream before returning to this potent switch word, "This is the Girl". One of the challenges when approaching the modus operandi of the dream-work is that all of these ploys encroach on and invade each other. Reading Freud, one can see that he himself found it difficult to make his way through this insistent intrication. Intricated but also distinguishable, these ploys are visible in *Mulholland Drive*.

Displacement

What Freud called "displacement" is a shifting of psychic intensities. The bits and pieces of memory that make it into the dream *are* its nevralgic points, not in themselves but as carriers—signifiers—of an acute impact on the dreamer which because now disguised can be revisited in a bearable manner. Actually, in Freud's view, the overall ostensible story of the dream simply reflects our tendency to narrativise, concealing the fact that the whole dream is a heap of isolated fragments which in Freud's words are "jammed up together like pack ice" (Freud, 1900a, p. 341) to create a tellable tale. In the analytic room, faced with a real dream, the analyst will recognise this and will see each fragment as carrying its own associative network. Lynch brilliantly shows that the random memories that make it into the dream are never random, but precisely because of their neutral status in the moment of occurrence are invested by the dreamer with the subjective intensity of that moment.

The dinner party sequence in the second part of the film contains several of the real-life intensities displaced in the dream. These displacements resulted from the successive humiliations to which Diane was subjected, registered here in her pain-spangled eyes. Her marginal noticing at each of these moments, of the coffee cup, the glance of the man opposite, and the Cowboy passing in the background will all make their way into the text of the dream. But as we can see in each instance, when they surface in the dream, displacement will not be enough, and will have to be reinforced with absurdity for this level of pain to gain entry to the dream.

The dream within the dream

Freud sees the dream within the dream as a kind of reinforced refusal of what has to be kept at bay. To dream that you are dreaming is to distance still more and render less real whatever it is you are dreaming. This happens three times in the early section of Diane's dream. There is a sense that this dream gets off to a shaky start. The dream-protagonist at the beginning is wounded, vulnerable, amnesiac, and this is the most fragmented, incoherent part of the dream, the part that veers most frequently into danger zones, apart from its final moments when the whole dream starts to implode. As the injured Rita (also Laura Harring) staggers through what looks like a Hollywood set, she hears an exact replication of the complicit couple-laughter of Adam (Justin Theroux) and Camilla at the dinner party, and immediately lies down and goes into a dream about a lesser threat, the two detectives. Then shortly after she makes it indoors, Aunt Ruth's search for her keys similarly comes too close to breaking the surface of the dream. Rita again goes to sleep and dreams a frightening allusion to the blue key, albeit one that is sufficiently indirect for her to go on dreaming. This of course is the Winkie's Diner dream, also weighted by displacement, since the massive turbulence and anxiety of the moment is all carried by the seemingly unimportant detail of this random guy who happened to be standing in Winkie's while Diane was engaging the assassin. This dream in turn morphs into a further enigmatic sequence of minatory telephone exchanges, culminating in the image of the red telephone used by Camilla to lure Diane to the party.

Each time there is a specific trigger in the dream, a too-threatening allusion, it breaks the narrative surface and necessitates an extraneous fragment. This fragment varies in its susceptibility to being integrated into what the dream has constructed as a tellable story. The third time the dream within the dream happens in *Mulholland Drive*, the trigger is the Hollywood dream itself. As a signifier, Hollywood as dream is omnipresent here. And in the way unconscious knowledge operates, it is at once that which weaves the texture of the dream as a not knowing and at the same time that which tears holes in this texture. Following directly on the series of strange telephone exchanges, a sunny, excited Betty bursts on the scene tingling with the euphoria of the Hollywood dream, and then twenty minutes later, when she proceeds to burble on about this to Rita, the mention of this particular dream sends Rita into a faint. It then provokes the longest narrative fragmentation, the one that is the least susceptible to integration and the most farcical foray into non-sense. This takes us to another ploy of the dream-work, which is absurdity.

Absurdity

As Freud says in *The Interpretation of Dreams*, devoting a whole section to it (Freud, 1900a, p. 426), absurdity is such a frequent feature in dreams that one has to take it seriously. He points out how often absurdity appears in the context of death and links it to another dream ploy: reversal. He also emphasises its link to emotional turbulence. Absurdity, according to Freud, indicates "the presence in the dream-thoughts of a particularly embittered and passionate polemic" (Freud, 1900a, p. 436), so one can assume that very specific intensities are at work when the dream spills over into farce. Furthermore, these overspills will be the most resistant to coherence, the least susceptible to being recuperated into meaningfulness.

The *Mulholland Drive* fan will of course immediately think of the ludicrously slapstick scene where Diane's hired killer shoots three people in the atmosphere of a domestic task gone tiresomely wrong, and the brief insert where we see a blonde, bruised prostitute reaching into his shirt pocket—home of the blue key. Freud suggests that dreams "are often most profound when they seem most crazy" (Freud, 1900a, p. 444). In real life, this is where the analyst will suspect the threatened breakthrough of a particularly dangerous allusion. There are three signifiers in *Mulholland Drive*, which, when they threaten to appear, shunt the dream into absurdity. These are the switch word "This is the Girl", the blue key, and sexual betrayal. Each of these provokes farce. But it is interesting that, as mentioned above, the most prolonged of these seems to be a dream within a dream provoked by the signifier Hollywood dream itself.

Following Rita's faint, as she drops into sleep, the scene cuts to an aerial shot of Hollywood before zoning in on its workings in a concentrate of displacement and absurdity in the wonderfully surreal director's meeting between Adam and the Castigliane brothers (Angelo Badalamenti and Dan Hedaya) in which the coffee cup and the repeated phrase "This is the Girl" lock ludicrously into each other. And even this is not quite enough. The attempted deviation, the avoidant fragment, is itself repeatedly pulled into the orbit of traumatic truth, so the question put to the enigmatic Mr Roque (Michael J. Anderson), "Do you mean shut everything down?" immediately recalls the final moment of the dreaming Diane's real-life exchange with the hired killer—his laughter when she asks what the blue key opens, segueing the dream by way of this laughter into even further absurdity as the hired killer, in a series of slapstick misadventures, exasperatedly has to kill two inconvenient interlopers as well as a buzzing vacuum cleaner.

Reversal

The third major trigger is sexual betrayal. Since none of these defensive ploys operate singly, this trigger cuts in at a moment when the dream seems to have found its stride by means of another modality of the dream-work: that of reversal. Where in real life Diane had been at Camilla's mercy, in the dream Betty takes the initiative as girl detective and the dream steadies up and becomes a lot less incoherent from then on, but at the first hint that the bond then forged could deepen into something else—the moment where they briefly hold hands—the dream signals the real-life outcome of this by breaking into a version of Adam's comic betrayal story. Once again, it is the triggering event that allows us to assess the incursion of absurdity, and permits us to recognise that what is being signalled carries a specific intensity.

One of the difficulties of working with dreams is that when they are least readable they are also closest to their core, the core that if known would make it impossible for the dreamer to go on being, to continue to inhabit the fantasy structure that supports their existence. And yet, as we see in *Mulholland Drive*, this impossible knowledge exercises a magnetic pull on all the tactics of avoidance that the dream has at its command, up until the point when the dreamer is indeed unable to go on dreaming. As the blue key is about to be inserted in the blue box, Betty vanishes from the dream, then the entire dream itself is plunged into the unplumbable and vorticial darkness of the opened box.

The film ends with the much more catastrophic real-life version of the subject unable to maintain her position as subject when the veil of unknowing is fatally torn open. As Diane allows herself bit by bit to remember the events leading up to the dream, she reaches the point where the hitman laughs at being asked what the key opens. In the dream, this memory broke open a fragment of unassimilable absurdity; in real life, the remembered laughter amplifies into shrieks of hallucinated mockery, propelling her into psychotic delusion and suicide.

Freud called the dream the "royal road" to the unconscious. Perhaps more than any other phenomenon it allows us to see the formal modalities by which our refusal to know becomes stained with that knowing. These formal modalities have proved difficult to replicate by other means. *Mulholland Drive*, exceptional in many respects, is also exceptional in this.

References

Freud, S. (1900a). *The Interpretation of Dreams. S. E.*, 4–5. London: Hogarth.

Lacan, J. (1991). *The Seminar of Jacques Lacan. Book II: The Ego in Freud's Theory and in the Technique of Psychoanalysis 1954–1955*. New York, NY: Norton.

CHAPTER 4

Lost angels in Los Angeles: Lynchian psychogenic fugues

Mary Wild

From the South Bay to the Valley
From the West Side to the East Side
Everybody's very happy
'Cause the sun is shining all the time
Looks like another perfect day
I love LA (We love it)
I love LA (We love it)
Look at that mountain
Look at those trees
Look at that bum over there, man
He's down on his knees
Look at these women
There ain't nothin' like 'em nowhere

Randy Newman

Los Angeles is sometimes spoken about in pejorative terms: shallow, phoney, attracting fakery and illusion (that's the stereotype). In terms of psycho-geography, every place has a unique and fascinating story to tell. And for the surrealist filmmaker David Lynch, the prospect of engaging with dark, underlying forces at the core of a pretty dream machine remains utterly irresistible.

Lynch loves the natural light in LA and appreciates how Hollywood's film business came to be the most successful in the world. There is something very special about California sunshine; everything that basks in that glow looks gorgeous; it has the power to seduce faithful followers of beauty, and even win over cynics with an aversion to the shallow side of the film industry. "The light in LA is so bright, it brings a feeling of creative freedom", Lynch has remarked. Actually he never stood a chance; putting up with showbiz charlatans was a sacrifice he was willing to make to fuse his projects with that precious luminosity! He has been a resident of Los Angeles for several decades now, painting in his studio, shooting films, falling in and out of favour with network executives, refusing to capitulate to demands that might place his creative vision at risk, resorting on occasion to self-financing in order to uphold the autonomy of his vision as an artist.

> *I love Los Angeles. I know a lot of people go there and they see just a huge sprawl of sameness. But when you're there for a while, you realize that each section has its own mood. The golden age of cinema is still alive there, in the smell of jasmine at night and the beautiful weather. And the light is inspiring and energizing. Even with smog, there's something about that light that's not harsh, but bright and smooth. It fills me with the feeling that all possibilities are available. I don't know why. It's different from the light in other places. The light in Philadelphia, even in the summer, is not nearly as bright. It was the light that brought everybody to L.A. to make films in the early days. It's still a beautiful place.*
>
> David Lynch, *Catching The Big Fish* (2006)

LA, with rolling hills, Rodeo Drive, art deco cinemas, star-studded boulevards, awards ceremonies, green juice bars, plastic surgeons, Bel Air mansions, psychedelic drugs scene, murderous cults, race riots, abject poverty, crooked cops, gang violence, out-of-work actors, empty promises, and shattered dreams; LA, with all its paradoxes and contradictions, peddling hope in the form of moving images, casting stars in career-defining roles, casting spells, casting couches … It's easy to see why a surrealist would be drawn to such an ultra-weird city.

In the summer of 1994, Lynch was glued to the tube as helicopters and police vehicles chased a white Bronco along California freeways. When O. J. Simpson was accused of double homicide, his televised trial riveted Lynch—the "not guilty" verdict shocked him, because he was convinced O. J. had committed those horrific crimes. What intrigued the filmmaker most was the question of denial—how could the famous sports star be capable of committing unspeakable carnage while maintaining a façade of innocence? How could he carry on playing golf, signing football jerseys and smiling, compartmentalising those awful events as if they never happened, keeping up the famous "O. J." persona in the face of public wrath? The ghosts of his estranged wife Nicole Brown Simpson and her male companion Ron Goldman haunted LA and the world over, but seemingly had no effect on the alleged murderer. Scotomisation—a refusal to see objective reality and radical rejection of intolerable facts, narrowing of the field of consciousness—is a concept that would attract the attention of most cinema auteurs … this bizarre psychological phenomenon is pure Lynchian territory!

One day, a producer came across a term in a medical journal that sent Lynch's imagination soaring: "psychogenic fugue", a short-lived reversible amnesia that follows a stressful or traumatic event, leading to the establishment of an entirely new identity. Often travel or wandering is featured in the disorder, where a subject is convinced that they are a new person, presenting a new name, and claiming a totally different backstory. When Lynch found out about this psychiatric term (which is no longer featured in the *Diagnostic and Statistical Manual of Mental Disorders*), his excitement went into overdrive. A theoretical fugue state resolves the mystery of odd behaviour, such as O. J.'s response during and after his murder trial—the mind attempts to flee a disturbing aspect of reality by any means necessary, even if it involves escaping only within the psyche's realm, and creating a new set of delusional facts to hide behind …

Lynch told a different version of the tragic O. J. Simpson saga in his 1997 release *Lost Highway*, the neo-noir psychological horror film starring Bill Pullman and Patricia Arquette. The story begins with a jazz musician, Fred, who suspects his enigmatic wife Renee of being unfaithful to him; certainly, their relationship appears to be cold and distant, but in Fred's mind everything his wife does and says confirms his theory that she is having an affair. He is plagued with jealousy and tormented by strange, nightmarish visions of terrible violence taking place inside the home he shares with Renee. Los Angeles represents a prominent idea in *Lost Highway*'s intrigue, the narrative delivering many tropes of the film noir genre, which was invented by Hollywood studios. Arquette perfectly embodies the glamorous *femme fatale* figure, the devouring woman who removes a status object from the leading man and castrates him allegorically. LA, like a deadly seductress, destroys victims with immense flair in *Lost Highway*. During a particularly disquieting scene, Fred comes face to face with a Mystery Man at a chic party; the extravagant cachet of the LA social scene serves as the perfect backdrop to uncanny, paranormal, and lethal aesthetics. Following an unexplained murder, iconic California freeways become the setting for manifestations of dread, fevered escape, and ghostly fugue into an altogether foreign consciousness. The final scene of *Lost Highway* is a direct reference to the O. J. Simpson police car chase—an ironic nod to what has become a notorious moment in the city's modern history.

Rita (Laura Harring) and Betty (Naomi Watts) in *Mulholland Drive* (2001), dir. Lynch, courtesy of BFI Stills, Posters and Designs

The fixation with Los Angeles is amplified in David Lynch's 2001 release *Mulholland Drive* starring Naomi Watts; here the theme of unrequited love moves from the context of domestic violence to the turbulent relationship between an aspiring actress and the Hollywood film industry itself. The very first scene takes place on the mountainside road with danger lurking at every turn; Mulholland Drive is known as the "road to stardom" because it leads to major film and TV studios in Burbank, California. As Stephen Holden observed in the *New York Times*: "The film is an ever-deepening reflection on the allure of Hollywood, multiple role-playing and self-invention that the movie-going experience promises". The traffic accident within the first few minutes sets the tone for the film: *Hollywood hurts*, and sometimes the pain leaves behind deep emotional scars. "I remember driving along on Mulholland Drive many times as a newcomer to LA, constantly getting rejected at auditions, sobbing my heart out in my car, going *What the Hell am I doing here*", Watts recalls. Her character initially appears to be called "Betty", a wide-eyed go-getter who sets out to take tinsel town by storm. But Lynch's film might be an inverted Cinderella story: will show business heavy hitters discover Betty? Or will someone else be chosen for the part?

In *Mulholland Drive*, Los Angeles is presented as a "dream place", perpetuating the myth of Hollywood as the ultimate land of opportunity. We see Betty gazing longingly at the entrance of a grand film studio—the birthplace of her forthcoming fame, perchance? Her *tour de force* audition earns her a meeting with a maverick director who is casting an important role in his new film. Their eyes meet from across the soundstage; Lynch frames this encounter as a romantic one: the viewer is invited to read the interaction between the ambitious star-to-be and the powerful Hollywood system as a whimsical love affair. As the film unfolds, however, it becomes clear that the city nicknamed "La-La Land" is actually an inscrutable, untrustworthy lover! Indeed, LA lures young hopefuls, makes false promises, breaks hearts ritualistically, and kills dreams without a shred of remorse. In *Mulholland Drive*, it is customary to see bleached-out shots of the characters superimposed on iconic images of Los Angeles—repeating the opening credit scene of Betty/Diane winning a jitterbug contest. Performers are represented as illusions, phantoms, lost angels ... like ghosts blurring over the urban jungle of the LA skyline, sacrificed by Hollywood and lost forever. By their very nature, films are simulated reality, and Lynch's surrealist vision confronts the traumatic quality of unrequited love between actors and the film industry.

In the final instalment of an apparent trilogy of LA-based films, Lynch converges the first two themes of non-reciprocated marital love and the heartbreak of an aspiring film star in his 2006 release *Inland Empire* (the title refers to a region in the periphery of greater Los Angeles). The plot revolves around Hollywood actress Nikki Grace (Laura Dern), who is cast to play the highly coveted film role of Susan Blue in *On High In Blue Tomorrows*—this is her long-awaited "comeback" role in the industry. To prove herself, she is determined to "become" the role, losing herself wholly in every aspect of the part; she even enters a piece of unfinished set design and becomes trapped in another story and another life. Soon Nikki and Susan's psyches become entangled, and the boundaries of identity proceed to blur beyond all rational comprehension; different versions of Nikki/Susan intersect and become indistinguishable from one another. The worlds of fiction and reality coexist simultaneously, so that it becomes almost impossible to separate the actress from the performance. Method acting stands in for the running theme of psychogenic fugue in *Inland Empire*, and it quickly becomes clear that only the love and identification of her faithful audience has the magical power to release her from the purgatorial jail of a fragmented identity (i.e. a way to "come back" from a soul-rupturing nightmare).

Inland Empire grew out of Lynch's lifelong obsession with Billy Wilder's 1950 iconic work of genius *Sunset Boulevard*, even co-opting some of its imagery and references. Nikki Grace is duty bound to carry out the disintegration of her identity, becoming a riddle for the audience, an urban ghost stalking the Hollywood Walk of Fame, and a neo-noir angel lost even to herself. We are compelled to regard Los Angeles in the position of the film director, casting an evil spell on Nikki; the wicked magician who saws her selfhood in half merely for the fleeting amusement of a fickle audience.

And yet it is via the method acting process that Nikki embarks on her path to "cinematic truth", as she dives within to investigate the psychological motives of the Susan Blue character, drawing on personal emotions and subjective memories to deliver a lifelike performance. In *Inland Empire*, method acting disfigures Nikki, breaks down her ontological security, links moments from her own experience to that of the role she's cast to play, where she imagines and inhabits Susan's consciousness completely. Success for Nikki is total immersion into art: a self-inflicted psychogenic fugue. Nikki Grace steps so far into character that her life in reality is confused (she appears to exhibit signs of psychosis). The parameters of identity become hazier; she has a real-life affair with her co-star Devon while their characters (Susan and Billy) have a romance on-screen. The audience's love is the only possible means to break the spell and restore identity … but will this come to pass?

Los Angeles is the perfect silent actor in Lynch's cinematic triptych—generating urban ghosts *ad infinitum*, evoking heaven and hell in the same frame, recalling stars of the Golden Age and inducting new ones, too. *Lost Highway*, *Mulholland Drive*, and *Inland Empire* are love letters to LA and urgent warnings in equal measure. We are reminded that the cinematic experience is also a type of psychogenic fugue, and maybe suspension of disbelief is cathartic because everyone has something they want to forget …

- *Father, do you believe in ghosts?*
- *Why, yes, my son!*
- *You do? I would not have thought so.*
- *Oh, not the human kind of ghost. No, not at all. But look up, boy, and see a sky full of them.*
- *The stars, Father? I do not follow.*
- *Every star is a sun as big, as bright as our own. Just imagine how far away from us you'd have to move the Sun, to make it appear as small and faint as a star! The light from the stars travels very fast, faster than anything, but not infinitely fast. It takes time for their light to reach us. For the nearest ones, it takes years. For others, centuries. Some stars are so far away, it takes eons for their light to get to Earth. By the time the light from some stars gets here, they are already dead. For those stars, we see only their ghosts. We see their light, but their bodies perished long, long ago.*

(A conversation between astronomer William Herschel and his son John.)

From the television series *Cosmos*, Season 1, Episode 4: "A Sky Full of Ghosts".

CHAPTER 5

"It's a strange world, isn't it?" A voyeuristic lens on David Lynch's *Blue Velvet**

Andrea Sabbadini

David Lynch's *Blue Velvet* (1986) is a coming-of-age story developed through a mixture of criminal and psychological investigations, transgressive sexuality, romantic love, and psychopathic violence—all presented in its auteur's unique filmic language. This is a language that appeals to our conscious curiosity to understand the movie's narrative plot and its characters' behaviour, but also invites us to relate them to our own deep-seated unconscious fears and desires.

Written and directed by Lynch in 1986, after such other original films as *Eraserhead* (1977), *The Elephant Man* (1980), and *Dune* (1984), *Blue Velvet* is a masterful work providing material sufficiently intense to deeply engage us spectators, both visually and emotionally, but so artfully created as to allow us to immerse ourselves in this material without becoming excessively disturbed by it.

In the process, this movie also explores (as *Mulholland Drive* (2001) will do fifteen years later) some unsavoury aspects of the underbelly of

---

* A shorter version of this chapter was originally published, in both Spanish and Portuguese, in Vol. 16, No 2, 2018, *Calibán, RLP*. It is reprinted with permission.

provincial American society, sometimes enriching its portrayal with ironic observations on family dynamics, in a space reminiscent of some of Edward Hopper's paintings of airless interiors. In Knafo and Feiner's words, Lynch "inverts the 'American dream'—the idealised vision of a comfortable, orderly, secure and moral life—and [...] undermines the illusion of goodness that bolsters one's security and comfort" (Knafo & Feiner, 2002, p. 1445). The resulting picture is one of the contrast between an artificial, superficial veneer of petit-bourgeois respectability and a world of unspeakable secrets festering underneath.

Blue Velvet opens on a blue velvet curtain covering the whole screen. The plot takes us to the small American town of Lumberton (imaginary, though a real one by that name does exist in North Carolina). Here Jeffrey Beaumont (played by Kyle MacLachlan), a young man described by Lynch as "both innocent and curious", returns from university to live with his mother and to manage his father's hardware store following his hospitalisation. Jeffrey's accidental discovery in the grass of a severed and bug-infested human ear leads to his meeting with the detective John Williams, who takes charge of the investigation, and with his daughter Sandy (Laura Dern). By eavesdropping on her father, Sandy finds out that cabaret singer Dorothy Vallens (Isabella Rossellini), a most unusual specimen of *femme fatale*, is suspected to be somehow involved in the mystery of the amputated ear. She shares this bit of intelligence with Jeffrey, and they go together to the Slow Club to hear Dorothy sing "Blue Velvet", a song made popular in the 1960s by Bobby Vinton. With Sandy's ambivalent collusion Jeffrey then intrudes into Dorothy's private space and personal life. Hidden inside a closet in her apartment, he witnesses Dorothy being verbally and sexually abused by criminal boss and psychopathic supremo Frank Booth (Dennis Hopper) who, having kidnapped her son and husband, uses his perverse powers to control her. Discovered by Frank, Jeffrey has then to bravely engage in some frightening confrontations with him. To further complicate matters, Jeffrey becomes erotically involved with Dorothy and romantically with Sandy, until the narrative gets resolved into a deliberately unconvincing "happy ending", and *Blue Velvet* closes on that same blue velvet curtain which had opened it.

I would like to suggest that the protagonists of *Blue Velvet* are "polymorphously perverse" adults, probably evolved from the "polymorphously perverse" children described in the second of Freud's *Three Essays on Sexuality* (Freud, 1905, p. 191). The word perversion is highly charged as well as intrinsically ambiguous. Sexual perversions refer to a variety of fantasies—from fetishism to necrophilia to the two-sided coins of voyeurism/exhibitionism and sado/masochism—fantasies sometimes played out in actual activities involving relationships with other people, but mostly relegated to the dark corners of one's unconscious mind.

Psychoanalysts working with perverse patients are used to experiencing in their own countertransference something either analogous or (more often) complementary to what their patients express, such as an excessive curiosity about their exhibitionistic activities or some unnecessary cruelty in the interpretation of their masochistic attitudes. This may be inevitable and, assuming the therapists will notice it and work through it within themselves rather than enacting it, it could represent an indispensable tool for the understanding of the patients' inner world.

Works of fiction often portray characters whose perverse desires—whether just imagined or explicitly played out—are significant aspects of their existence: in books, on the stage, or on the screen. Focusing here just on cinema, countless films seem to have as their main purpose that of exciting, confusing, or frightening their spectators. Some auteurs, however, such as, among others: Alfred Hitchcock (*Psycho*, 1960); Michael Powell (*Peeping Tom*, 1960); Luis Buñuel (*Belle de Jour*, 1967); Bernardo Bertolucci (*Luna*, 1979); Pedro Almodóvar (*Matador*, 1986); and Michael Haneke (*Hidden*, 2005), have explored the theme of perversion and its complexities with special subtlety, courage, and originality. Their movies, I suggest, induce in their viewers a certain amount of identification with the perverse side of the characters they portray, but also allow spectators to take some distance from them and to reflect on the meaning of their behaviour rather than become overwhelmed by it. In the process, viewers may be induced to challenge, or at least reconsider, their own preconceived ideas and moral attitudes.

This, I think, also applies to Lynch's *Blue Velvet*, a movie pervaded throughout by perversions. Sandy eavesdrops on her father's private conversations about suspects connected with the cut-off ear; Jeffrey voyeuristically spies on Dorothy's erotic activities from the louvre door inside a closet; Dorothy expresses her own masochistic need, having succeeded in seducing Jeffrey, to get him to physically hurt her; Frank indulges in verbal and bodily sadistic attacks on Dorothy and on anyone else in his proximity. The whole atmosphere of the film, and the behaviours of its protagonists, are profoundly perverse. We could even suggest that Lynch himself is playing perverse games with his spectators by luring them (us) inside the "strange world" inhabited by his characters.

Of the several forms of perversions explicitly portrayed (such as Dorothy's masochism and Frank's sadism) or just alluded to (such as Frank's fetishism for blue velvet material), I would like to focus on the one which I believe runs through, and to some extent structures, the whole film: voyeurism (and, by implication, its complementary side, exhibitionism). This is of special significance for us, insofar as movies are predominantly objects of "visual pleasure" (Mulvey, 1975), and our love of them always involves an amount of curiosity likely to be a recurrence of the one for the "mysteries" of sexuality and procreation originally experienced earlier in our lives.

Elsewhere I have suggested that the term voyeurism describes what are in fact two phenomena, different though not always easily distinguishable, which I have called *covert* and *collusive*. "Covert voyeurism", I wrote,

> is a narcissistic form of penetrative aggression directly related to primal scene fantasies and it involves gratification through the watching of objects who are themselves unaware of being watched [...] Collusive voyeurism, on the other hand, involves the experience of pleasure through the activity of watching objects who are well aware that they are being watched [...] This is a more sophisticated form of perversion because it implies some recognition that others are not just extensions of one's own self, but real persons responding to the voyeuristic activities of the subject and potentially getting themselves exhibitionistic satisfaction from being looked at.
>
> (Sabbadini, 2014a, p. 103)

In response to Jeffrey's telling inspector Williams that he is "real curious" about the severed ear, Sandy's eavesdropping on her father's conversation about it, a scene not shown in the film but implied by what happens next, is an instance of covert voyeurism. Jeffrey's watching Dorothy being forced into a ritualised sexual encounter with Frank is an instance of collusive voyeurism: Dorothy is well aware of Jeffrey's presence in the closet, and Jeffrey is well aware that she is well aware of it; but it is also an example of covert scopophilia insofar as Frank does not know of Jeffrey's hidden presence in the room. Excited and horrified in equal measure, like a child exposed to the primal scene in the parental bedroom, Jeffrey watches on, and we with him, as the fixed camera's position invites us to identify with him. It could be argued that both Jeffrey (who had to hide in order to avoid being discovered by Frank) and Dorothy (who had to submit to Frank's abusing and raping her) were forced to create such a voyeuristic/exhibitionistic scenario, rather than having voluntarily constructed it for their own sexual pleasure. However, it is clear that, even if it wasn't originally their conscious choice, both Jeffrey and Dorothy get some perverse gratification from finding themselves in that situation.

It would be easy to describe Dorothy as Frank's "sex slave" as we learn that he can control her by holding her husband and son hostage. We watch him violently abusing her, his face distorted in a grotesque sneer (one that could have been imagined by Francis Bacon) and covered by a mask through which he breathes amyl nitrate, a drug inducing a state of euphoria and visual hallucinations. But his sadistic and drug-fuelled sexuality is complementary to Dorothy's masochistic association of pleasure with pain; while Frank is raping her, Lynch's camera closes up on the almost ecstatic expression on her face. Soon after this scene we watch Dorothy seducing Jeffrey and begging him to: "*Hit me, hit me, HIT ME!*". Presumably, she could only reach orgasm, for reasons likely to originate from some childhood traumatic experiences, when getting hurt and feeling humiliated. Jeffrey, reluctant at first and guilty afterwards, complies with her request, realising perhaps that "the condition for his sexual initiation entails his acceptance of his sadistic impulses" (Knafo & Feiner, 2002, p. 1448).

As a means to gratify these various forms of perverse sexuality, power plays an important part. The power of brute violence (Frank's abusive behaviour and foul language), the power of threats (Dorothy, wearing a blue velvet dressing gown, holds a carving knife in her right hand while sliding her left one inside Jeffrey's underpants), the power stemming from inducing fear in others in order either to control and dominate them or to obtain what they want from them: something that tyrants are well aware of, whether they are despots in dictatorial regimes or, like Frank, bosses of criminal gangs.

But what about the tyrannical power of *internal* fears, of those cruel, controlling forces which dominate the minds of individuals and make them slaves to paranoid fantasies? Often going unnoticed to others, the power of such persecutory fantasies can dramatically create for those affected by them the terrifying experience of living in hell. This may even apply to the world inhabited by Frank himself—a paranoid, psychotic inner universe which he can only survive by forcibly projecting it onto others. One aspect of it is his incapacity to think in other-than-concrete terms; for instance, he can only understand in such terms the metaphorical meaning of the "blue velvet" in Dorothy's signature song. We see him fetishistically caressing a piece of blue velvet material when listening to her singing in the Slow Club, later placing the blue velvet belt of her dressing gown in his own mouth and in her mouth while raping her, and having pushed yet another blue velvet cloth in the mouth of her murdered husband—the man, we only then discover, whose left ear had been cut off. Shot by Jeffrey, Frank dies holding Dorothy's dressing gown across his arm.

With reference to Freud's view about "two currents whose union is necessary to ensure a completely normal attitude in love" (Freud, 1912d, p. 180), Bodin and Poulsen consider *Blue Velvet* "a psychological tale about the young man Jeffrey's attempt to find a solution in which the two currents of affection and sensuality form a synthesis and thus resolve his Oedipus complex [...] out from an infantile sexuality towards a genital sexuality" (Bodin & Poulsen, 1994, p. 166). Other psychoanalytic authors who have written about our film also focus on Jeffrey's attempts to deal with his as-yet unresolved oedipal issues. Sekoff suggests that

> the signs and symbols of our dream-film boldly point to an oedipal drama. So boldly—with its broken fathers, beckoning women, forbidden desires and castrative threats—that the dream-text seems transparent [...] When Sandy asks Jeffrey, 'Are you a pervert or a detective?', she knowingly points us to the latent structure of the dream narrative. It is a rhetorical question, for we can see that the detective's search will embody a perverse solution.
>
> (Sekoff, 1994, p. 423)

Jeffrey, I would add, is *both* a detective and a pervert, insofar as we could speculate that all detectives are also perverts (so to speak). Here, then, Sandy's question would relate not just to Jeffrey, but also to her own father, who had chosen the detection of crimes as his professional activity—perhaps an instance of sublimation. Incidentally, the sublimation of sexual and aggressive tendencies into socially acceptable endeavours is involved in many honourable human activities and professional choices: the unconscious transformation of original sadistic impulses into life-saving surgical operations, the display of exhibitionistic trends through brilliant acting performances on stage or screen, the displacement of fantasies about rescuing ourselves from our own unresolved psychological conflicts into successful psychotherapeutic work with patients …

At the beginning of *Blue Velvet*, we watch the tragi-comical scene in which Jeffrey's father becomes incapacitated following a stroke while watering his garden. Campbell and Campbell (2019) believe that a central element in the film is the representation of Jeffrey's primal scene fantasies in the absence of a father who could protect the incest boundaries and help him mediate the "strange world" in which he finds himself. It is left to Frank, a psychopathically violent adult male, to fill "the psychic hole that is left by the absence of a paternal guardian of the incest barrier in the film. Psychically, when there is no symbolisation of the primal scene, we regress to a psychotic level of functioning and enact incestuous wishes and parental retaliation" (Campbell & Campbell, 2019, p. 2).

Knafo and Feiner add that "as with Oedipus, whose need to penetrate the riddle of the sphinx led him to uncover his own crimes, Jeffrey's investigations into the dark 'under-inner-world' lead him to find the same darkness within himself" (Knafo & Feiner, 2002, p. 1445).

Jeffrey's attempt to solve a mystery is then also a search for his own identity and masculinity, a search which brings him close to the affectionate "Madonna" Sandy, as well as to the seductive "Whore" Dorothy, the perverted victim whom he tries to rescue with his love for her. "*Hurt me!*" she begs him. "*No, I want to help you!*", he naively replies. Rescue fantasies, incidentally, are powerful motivators in many intimate relationships (psychoanalytic ones included), and often provide films with interesting plots (Sabbadini, 2014b, pp. 80–89).

The severed ear that Jeffrey finds in a field demands some further reflections. It could be considered as just a kind of Hitchcockian

MacGuffin, having as its only function to set in motion the events which follow, but being otherwise insignificant in itself. However, the fact that, of all possible objects, what Jeffrey finds half-hidden in the grass is a *body part* (and not, for instance, a shotgun or a briefcase full of dollars) charges it with special emotional connotations, for him and for the film's viewers. Indeed, such an object is "a fairly substantial reminder that castration can become reality. If an ear can be cut off, so can other parts of the body" (Bodin & Poulsen, 1994, p. 166).

Psychoanalysts use the term "part objects" with reference to the earliest forms of relationships that a baby entertains with others. It is only when a child can experience the existence of, say, a mother behind that prototypical part object which is her feeding breast, that full objects can begin to emerge for him; and even then, the "other", entirely "good" when present and satisfying his needs, is experienced as a different object from the "bad" one when it is absent or unresponsive. It will only be later in the child's development, when he manages to tolerate the ambivalent realisation that it is the same one love object who can be "good" at times and "bad" at other times, that he can begin to engage in full object relationships.

What I am suggesting here is that part objects, including the cut-off ear found by Jeffrey, can induce in those who come across them later in life (our film's protagonist, but also us, its spectators) a state of regressive, primitive, unconscious anxiety that would stem from their origins in the history of our human development. An instance, perhaps, of that disturbing phenomenon identified by Freud as "the uncanny" (1919h), the definition of which as "not simply a feeling of strangeness or alienation, [but] a peculiar commingling of the familiar and unfamiliar" (Royle, 2003, p. 1) may well apply to much of David Lynch's work.

Movies, many of them in the horror genre, that induce such anxiety in their viewers by showing them macabre images of severed body parts are too many to be listed here. I shall only mention the eye being sliced with a razor blade and the hand with ants crawling out from a hole in Buñuel and Dalí's surrealistic classic *Un Chien Andalou* (1929); the castrated penis in the erotic Japanese masterpiece *Ai no korida* [*In the Realm of the Senses*] (Nagisa Ōshima, 1976); and the cut-off head found in a box in Liliana Cavani's *Il portiere di notte* [*The Night Porter*] (1974) as well as in Joel and Ethan Coen's *Barton Fink* (1991)—a film aesthetically similar to much of Lynch's own work.

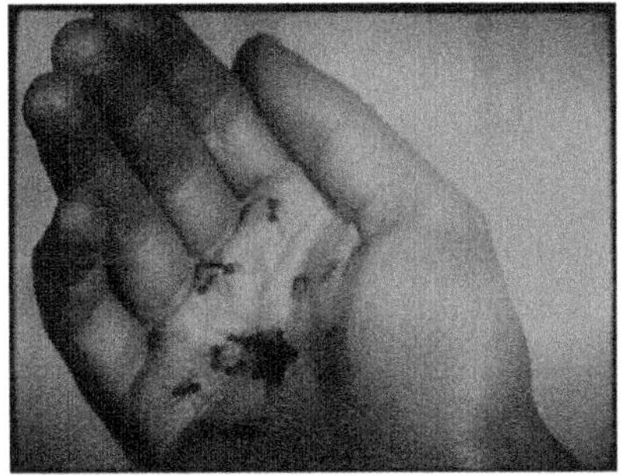

Hand with ants from *Un Chien Andalou* (1929), dirs. Buñuel and Dalí; Ear from *Blue Velvet* (1986), dir. Lynch

Not an eye, a hand, a penis, or a head in *Blue Velvet*, but … an ear! Such as the one, if I can freely associate here, missing from van Gogh's head in his 1889 self-portrait, or that of the 16-year-old Paul Getty III, cut off by his abductors in 1973 and sent to his family to put pressure on them to pay the ransom—unlike the one in *Blue Velvet* which, abandoned as it is in a field, does not seem to have any other purpose than to be evidence of someone's gratuitous, sadistic cruelty.

Vincent van Gogh, *Self-Portrait with Bandaged Ear*, 1889, oil on canvas, Courtauld Gallery, London. Image credit: Courtauld Institute

I believe that the general significance of ears rests on the importance of the earliest experience of hearing in the formation of a child's sense of identity. In parallel to the visual "mirroring" described by Winnicott (1967), the holding auditory reflection of the child's voice, sounds, and noises (a process I call "echoing") will allow the child not just to produce sounds, but also to learn to listen to them, enjoy them, and recognise them as his own. For echoing to take place, the empathic and containing voice of his carers is an indispensable sounding board to the child's voice. Only by being talked and listened to by those who love her will the child feel sufficiently supported to learn to listen to herself and thus gradually develop an individual identity. Well-functioning ears (the child's own and those of her carers) are essential body parts for such processes to occur (Sabbadini, 2014a, p. 126).

While films, unlike psychoanalysis, provide us primarily with visual experiences, their auditory components are also important, whether they consist of conversations, noises, or music (Dorothy is a singer). Indeed, it has been rightly suggested that "watching *Blue Velvet* is like listening to the patient's free associations not knowing where they are going, or what is behind the patient's words" (Campbell & Campbell, 2019, p. 9). Is Lynch, by choosing an ear as the missing body part in his film, also trying to tell us something about cinema, about one of the organs involved in its reception? In fact, he does not just show us, and more than once, the severed ear, but there are also two sequences in which his camera first zooms inside the canal of that cut-off organ (at the beginning of Jeffrey's amateurish investigation) and then zooms out of Jeffrey's own ear (at the end of his hellish journey)—almost as if it was inside this internal organ, and inside the protagonist's mind, that the whole narrative had taken place.

I suspect that Lynch got involved in the story of *Blue Velvet*, and so taken by his need to tell it in the visual language so distinctively his own (if not indifferent to other well-established genres, such as film noir and, occasionally, comedy), that he was not too bothered about its reception. In fact, the film was a flop at the box office before being recognised as a masterpiece by critics and becoming a cult movie for many of its viewers. In this respect, Pauline Kael described it as an inquiry into "the mystery and madness hidden in the 'normal'" (Kael, 1986), while Sekoff critically suggests that "*Blue Velvet* enters popular culture as another fetish—a commodity fetish that allows the purchase of an experience of the 'dark side' of life" (Sekoff, 1994, p. 437).

Lynch is a visionary, intuitive rather than intellectual filmmaker who, as actor Kyle MacLachlan has observed, "trusts his unconscious" and makes his choices based on it. As a result, his storytelling style is often free associative and requires from us viewers a complementary attitude of free-floating attention, or suspended disbelief, analogous to that familiar to those of us sitting behind an analytic couch. Here and there we have to allow ourselves to relinquish our wish to follow the logic of the story and rationally understand the development of the narrative in order to accept its "primary process" quality, to appreciate the original, artistic form in which it is presented, and even to enjoy its uncanny, perverse beauty. We can then find ourselves in a sort of dreamlike (or nightmare-like) space, such as Dorothy's dimly-lit, purple-coloured, and womb-like apartment number 710, or the rooms where Frank's associates guard their kidnapped hostages. Spaces, these ones, fascinating as they are mysterious, which made Dennis Hopper describe *Blue Velvet* as "the first American surrealist film".

As both Jeffrey and Sandy state more than once: "*It's a strange world, isn't it?*" Strange indeed! Thank you, David Lynch, for reminding us.

References

Bodin, G. & Poulsen, I. (1994). Psychic Conflicts in Contemporary Language: An Analysis of the Film *Blue Velvet* by David Lynch. *Scandinavian Psychoanalytic Review* 17(2): 159–177.

Campbell, D. & Campbell, C. (2019). Discussion of *Blue Velvet. Unpublished paper.*

Freud, S. (1905d). *Three Essays on the Theory of Sexuality. S. E.*, 7. London: Hogarth Press.

Freud, S. (1912d). On the Universal Tendency to Debasement in the Sphere of Love. *S. E., 11*. London: Hogarth Press.

Freud, S. (1919h). The "Uncanny". *S. E.*, 17. London: Hogarth Press.

Kael, P. (1986). *Blue Velvet*: Out There and In Here. *The New Yorker*, 22 September 1986.

Knafo, D. & Feiner, K. (2002). *Blue Velvet*: David Lynch's Primal Scene. *International Journal of Psychoanalysis* 83(6): 1445–1451.

Mulvey, L. (1975). Visual Pleasure and Narrative Cinema. *Screen* 16(3): 6–18.

Royle, N. (2003). *The Uncanny*. Manchester: Manchester University Press.

Sabbadini, A. (2014a). *Boundaries and Bridges: Perspectives on Time and Space in Psychoanalysis*. London: Karnac.

Sabbadini, A. (2014b). *Moving Images: Psychoanalytic Reflections on Film*. London: Routledge.

Sekoff, J. (1994). *Blue Velvet*: The Surface of Suffering. *Free Associations* 4(3): 421–446.

Winnicott, D. W. (1967). Mirror-role of Mother and Family in Child Development. In: *Playing and Reality*. London: Tavistock, 1971.

CHAPTER 6

The fragmented case of the Lynchian hysteric

Jamie Ruers

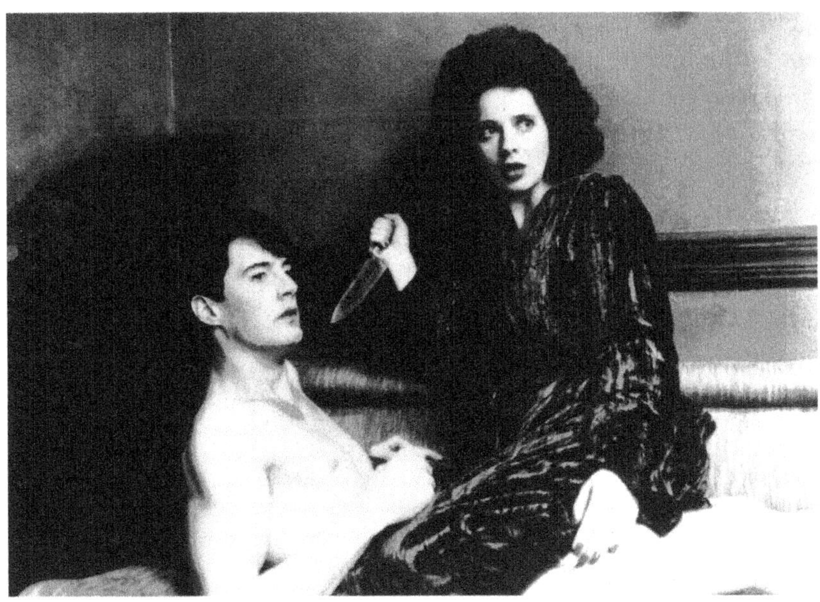

Jeffrey Beaumont and Dorothy Vallens in *Blue Velvet* (1986), dir. Lynch, courtesy of BFI Stills, Posters and Designs

Riddled with incoherent narratives, symbols, and otherworldly presences, David Lynch's cinema is one to be deciphered. Hardly any other element opens up so many questions as to his representations of women, which has been one of the most controversial and sometimes even divisive aspects of his films. However, this chapter will introduce a particular type of Lynchian female character—the hysteric. By using a formalist and aesthetic approach, we will attempt to situate Lynch's hysterical characters in the context of Freud and the wider history of psychoanalysis.

It is recounted in Ernest Jones' biography of Sigmund Freud that he famously asked his analysand and colleague, Princess Marie Bonaparte:

> The great question that has never been answered, and which I have not yet been able to answer, despite my thirty years of research into the feminine soul, is "What does woman want?"
>
> (Jones, 1955, p. 468)

The cinema of David Lynch also appears concerned with what women really want; from Dorothy Vallens (Isabella Rossellini) in *Blue Velvet* (1986) to Laura Palmer (Sheryl Lee) in *Twin Peaks* (1990–1991), to name a few. In Lynch's portrayal of women, there always appears to be a more subversive side to their character, as The Man from Another Place (Michael J. Anderson) once said: "She is filled with secrets". I suggest these characters bear qualities similar to the psychoanalytic model of hysteria. But what makes these particular characters so vivid in Lynch's work? Are there quintessential tropes that allow the spectator to identify them?

Hysteria: who's that girl?

Let us first establish the etymology of "hysteria". The term derives from the Greek word "hyster" meaning "womb". For Hippocrates and the ancient Greeks, hysteria was the result of a wandering womb. It was believed to move around the body in search of something, resulting in pains, swelling, and erratic behaviour. It was considered to be an inherently female condition. This belief continued well into the eighteenth century until the physician Philippe Pinel famously struck the chains of women who were locked up in the Bicêtre Hospital. He developed a more humane approach to the care of psychiatric patients, having moved away from bodily ailments for hysteria and begun investigations into scientific psychiatry.

Eugène Pirodon, *A Clinical Lesson of Dr Charcot at the Salpêtrière* (*Une leçon clinique du Dr Charcot à la Salpêtrière)*, after André Brouillet's oil painting of 1887, 1887–1899, lithograph, courtesy of Freud Museum London

Further research into the condition continued in the nineteenth century and came to the fore with French neurologist Jean-Martin Charcot. He led research in hypnosis and hysteria at the Salpêtrière Hospital, one of the leading hospitals in neurology with one of the first-ever neurology wards in the world. Charcot was known to present his patients exhibiting hysterical symptoms, such as fainting, having fits, or talking in tongues, to rooms of his colleagues. He believed hysteria was hereditary, and the symptoms were triggered later in life. His research was furthered by his student, Sigmund Freud, who studied under him in Paris from 1886 to 1887. It was through this early research into hysteria that Freud began to develop psychoanalysis. In the 1890s, he had published case studies on hysterical patients with his colleague Josef Breuer, investigating its unusual symptoms and possible remedies.

The symptoms of hysteria manifest in the body. In the nineteenth century, these symptoms were characterised by otherwise unexplained bodily functions, such as aches, pains, swelling, memory loss, speaking in different languages or tongues, lack of speech, convulsions, hallucinations, and perversions. The list goes on to include various other extreme or deviant behaviour (Hustvedt, 2011, pp. 4–8). Freud and Breuer concluded that the common factor in their hysterical patients was the experience of a moment of trauma from which these symptoms arose, stating, "*Hysterics suffer mainly from reminiscences*" (Freud & Breuer, 1895d, p. 7). Freud had found the patient's trauma was often experienced during their sexual development in childhood.

The modern-day perception of hysteria in psychoanalysis has developed into something quite different. Freud's investigations were followed by the research of French psychoanalyst Jacques Lacan from the 1930s onwards. Lacan divided neuroses into three categories: phobia, obsessional neurosis, and hysteria. The obsessional and the hysteric are most commonly placed as binary counterparts, as they are defined by their impossible desires: the obsessional's ambition is to close himself off to the possibility of incompleteness; the hysteric, on the other hand, believes their existence is contingent upon the Other, striving to be the Other's missing piece, who is often represented by a partner or lover. This is a common neurosis, and many people (regardless of gender) display varying degrees of hysteria.

Hysteria is stigmatised today in popular culture. It is still predominantly represented by extreme psychotic episodes and a steep decline in the mental stability of the character in question, who is more often than not female. Hysterical representations in major films include Blanche DuBois (Vivien Leigh) in *A Streetcar Named Desire* (1951) or Daisy Randone (Brittany Murphy) in *Girl, Interrupted* (1999). These particular examples bear an aesthetic similarity to Charcot's pre-psychoanalytic photographs, which we will return to later in this chapter. With this in mind, how far can we suggest the Lynchian model of the hysteric mirrors the psychoanalytic model, or does Lynch simply follow the cinematic tradition in his depictions of hysteria?

Dorothy Vallens: where two worlds collide

In the biographical 2016 film *David Lynch: The Art Life* (dir. Nguyen, Barnes, Neergaard-Holms), Lynch discusses his childhood, his early life as an artist, and some significant events that helped to shape him and his interdisciplinary work. In the documentary, he recalls a disturbing childhood memory from his time living in suburban Idaho, featuring the figure of a woman in emotional and physical despair. He says:

> It was one night, in the fall, it seemed to be pretty late. I don't know what we were doing but from across Shoshone Avenue, out of the darkness, comes something like a strange dream because I'd never seen an adult woman naked and she had beautiful pale white skin and she was completely naked and I think her mouth was bloodied. She came walking strangely across Shoshone Avenue and into Park Circle Drive. It seemed like she was a giant. And she came closer and closer and *my brother started to cry*. Something was wrong with her. And I don't know what happened but I think she sat down on the kerb crying. But it was very mysterious like we were seeing something *otherworldly* and I wanted to do something for her but I was little, I didn't know what to do. And I don't remember any more than that.

The figure that Lynch talks about in this early memory is one that he returns to in his cinematic work. It is without a doubt that he alludes to this scene most prominently in *Blue Velvet* in the character of Dorothy Vallens, who is represented in an almost identical way: a naked, bloodied, beaten, sexualised figure of a woman, on the backdrop of a peaceful, idyllic street in small-town America where the episode takes place. How does Lynch arrive at this shocking scene in *Blue Velvet*?

Blue Velvet tells the story of a young man named Jeffrey Beaumont (Kyle MacLachlan) who goes on a quest to solve the mystery of a found severed ear. A few minutes into the film, we meet Jeffrey's love interest Sandy Williams (Laura Dern), who states "We live in a strange world". However, what *Blue Velvet* actually presents is two worlds colliding: one is the homely yet patriarchal Lumberton, America, introduced in the opening scene with white picket fences in picture-perfect suburbia;

the second is its doppelgänger, the netherworld of the city, filled with corruption, kidnapping, rape, and murder. As Laura Mulvey has asserted, this netherworld is the uncanny double of Lumberton and represents a metaphor for the unconscious (Mulvey, 1996, p. 137).

The youthful, virginal character, Sandy Williams, represents a humanised product of the suburban utopia, and her binary counterpart is Dorothy Vallens, who first appears seductively performing a rendition of Bobby Vinton's "Blue Velvet" in a nightclub. Initially, Jeffrey is firmly placed as part of Sandy's small-town America but finds himself becoming entwined with Dorothy's world after breaking into her apartment one night.

As Dorothy arrives home, he hides in her closet and watches her. The spectator witnesses the scene from Jeffrey's position through the slats in the closet door. We watch Dorothy in her most vulnerable state: getting undressed, taking off her wig, on the phone bargaining with a correspondent, crying on the floor over her kidnapped child, all the while wearing a sultry robe and tantalising lingerie. She is the ideal scopic object as Jeffrey observes without being observed—there is no challenge to his gaze.

When she realises Jeffrey's hiding place, she drags him out and forces him to undress at knifepoint. Knafo and Feiner describe her as the "phallic, castrating (she wields a knife) maternal figure and identifies with her tormentors as she sadistically taunts Jeffrey" (Feiner & Knafo, 2002, p. 1447). The dynamic of this scene exhibits an uneasy contradiction for Jeffrey. It is both sexually arousing, as indicated by his pleasurable expression, all the while the risk of castration is also present. He acts on his desires by trying to touch her, but she screams "Don't touch me!" There is a conflict in Dorothy's actions. She refuses his affection but extends his longing. McGowan states that Dorothy is the embodiment of desire; she draws men to her: "They want to discover the secret of her desire, what it is that she wants, and the fact that she wants nothing, that nothing can satisfy her, compels them all the more" (McGowan, 2007, p. 99).

Understanding Dorothy becomes more complicated upon the entrance of a third character: Frank Booth (Dennis Hopper), whose bone-chilling arrival with an oxygen tank is followed by violent abuse and the rape of Dorothy. All the while, Jeffrey voyeuristically looks on, silently playing out his own perversions, observing the primal scene. As Frank hits Dorothy, the expression on her face is almost one of euphoria, of absolute pleasure, offering an unexpected response to such violent action. The spectator is now invited to ask questions: Is she being assaulted, or does she consent to this? Is she the violated mother, or is she the fantasist in this scenario? We believe we have two realms of desire to contend with—Jeffrey's infantile perversions witnessing the primal scene, and Frank's sadism. However, in *The Pervert's Guide to Cinema* (2009), Žižek offers another understanding to this scene:

> One should risk a more shocking and obverse interpretation: What if the central problem of this entire scene is Dorothy's passivity? What if what Frank is doing is a desperate, ridiculous but nonetheless effective attempt to help Dorothy, to awaken her out of her lethargy to bring her into life? So maybe if Frank is anyone's fantasy, maybe he is Dorothy's fantasy.

The hysteric in psychoanalysis is presented as a figure of uncertainty for others and even for herself. Lacan theorised that the hysteric questions "What does the Other want?" If the hysteric perpetually fantasises that it is herself that the Other is missing, she then places herself in the position of the object of desire for the Other. In *Introductory Lectures on Lacan*, Gessert suggests that the hysterical subject "attempts to sustain the Other's desire not simply by offering herself as a tantalising object, but by offering herself as an object that keeps slipping away, thus ensuring a lack of satisfaction and continuation of desire" (Gessert, 2014, pp. 63–64).

So we observe Dorothy performing as an object of desire for both Frank and Jeffrey. When Frank hits Dorothy, knowing that *he* experiences pleasure by doing so, she is imagining herself completing his sadistic fantasy, despite the expense of her own well-being. She later tells Jeffrey in a passionate moment: "I want you to hurt me". He refuses, so she says "Then go". She presents a finality, and as aforementioned, she is constantly slipping away. McGowan reasserts this as she performs because "she doesn't know what she wants and the performance leaves open the question of what Dorothy actually desires" (McGowan, 2007, p. 100). We realise the aim of Dorothy's desire is indeed perpetually in question. Therefore, we find ourselves constantly asking Freud's famous phrase: "What does woman want?"

The final scene with Dorothy is the most uncanny moment the film has to offer. Jeffrey and Sandy drive to Jeffrey's house to find Dorothy standing naked and bloodied on his front porch. The two worlds collide as Jeffrey's binary objects of desire finally meet. The serenity presented in the early scenes in Lumberton amplify what we now witness from Dorothy. It becomes clear that she has been seriously assaulted by Frank, leading her to behave in a hysterical manner. In her shaken state, Dorothy exclaims, "He put his disease in me". Dorothy's use of language here is symptomatic of her breakdown. The way she describes her sexual encounter with Jeffrey aligns the intimate act of sex with something as revolting as illness, a precursor for death. Therefore, there is a misdirection in the phrase, "He put his disease in me". She seeks out Jeffrey, full of desire, but presents herself to him as a deteriorating harbinger of death.

In Lynch's childhood memory mentioned previously, he describes an encounter with the woman in the street as "otherworldly". Here we see the same application of this term upon Dorothy as she is a by-product of Jeffrey's oedipal fantasy, displaced in idyllic suburbia. Dorothy is then involuntarily extracted from the suburban world of white picket fences and nuclear families, strapped to a hospital bed—an implication that she is being sectioned. She is portrayed as a victim of Frank's abuse in the netherworld, but now also a victim of the idyllic too. The uncanny encounter of the two worlds is expressed in the devoured body of the hysterical woman.

Cases: Lynch's "The Girl" and Charcot's "Augustine"

The Lynchian hysteric is not confined to *Blue Velvet*. The representation of the physical hysterical body is present in a much earlier work by Lynch, in a piece called *The Alphabet* (1968). This four-minute short, starring Lynch's first wife, Peggy, animates Lynch's personal conflict with language, which emerges as a key theme throughout Rodley's interview-biography, *Lynch on Lynch* (2005).

It is natural for the spectator to insist on finding a linear narrative, although this short film hardly possesses one. We can attempt to piece together a concept through its surreal symbols. It demonstrates a young woman—known simply as The Girl—in bed dreaming or fantasising about letters of the alphabet which appear to give birth to one another, supplemented by a sinister soundtrack of operatic singing.

This is followed by a scene of an animated phallic figure that emerges then morphs into the shape of a humanoid woman. Its head then implodes, and blood pours over itself. A distorted face appears on the screen, which says the only spoken line in the film: *Please remember you are dealing with the human form*. Suddenly, we return to The Girl in bed, who appears terrified beyond belief. Upon her traumatic awakening, The Girl reaches for the letters of the alphabet which appear around her but cannot touch them. She expresses horror but longing for them. Her intentions are unclear; her desire is incoherent. It draws to a close as The Girl violently vomits blood over the white sheets that she lays in.

This short, basic description of the film eliminates much of its evocation. It is haunting and shares many visual similarities with the medical photographs of the Salpêtrière Hospital in the late nineteenth century. One of the most famous case studies from this period was a patient of Charcot,

Paul-Marie-Léon Regnard, *Attitudes Passionnelles Extase*, 1878, printed photograph, courtesy of Getty Images

known simply as Augustine by the medical journals. She was admitted to the hospital at the young age of 15 years old for having hysterical fits: She hallucinated seeing swarms of rats, she lost her speech (aphonia), she writhed in pain, and she contorted her face and body. It was later discovered that she had been subject to a recurrent sexual trauma that began at the age of thirteen. She was raped by a family friend, a scene that she was said to hallucinate and re-enact during her hysterical fits. Her mother knew but did not act upon it, so Augustine was left to struggle in silence and developed severe hysterical symptoms (Hustvedt, 2011, p. 191). They manifested in the form of physical attacks, namely convulsions.

Photographs of Augustine's isolated symptoms led her to become a sort of poster girl in the twentieth century for hysteria. The French surrealist group of the 1920s–1930s even appropriated her image in their periodical, *Minotaure* with the caption, *Attitudes Passionnelles* (Passionate Attitudes). The image of the young woman having hysterical fits in bed recalls other classic films, such as *The Exorcist* (1973). This is unsettling for the spectator because a seemingly innocent figure is possessed by something from another world. Lynch has recreated this uncanny pairing of the young woman and destructive behaviour that has ceaselessly terrified generations of audiences.

The question of gender returns a few times throughout the short, beyond the fact that the only character's name, The Girl, is defined by her gender. Whilst gender itself is not an essential feat of hysteria in psychoanalysis—as the condition is not limited to one gender but has historically been associated with the female condition—the concept of gender situates oneself in relation to the other. The letters' giving birth to one another is a reminder of one's ability to be pregnant, to be a mother or not. Miller theorises that "The truth in a woman, in Lacan's sense, is measured by her subjective distance from the position of motherhood. To choose to be a mother [...] is to choose to exist as Woman" (Miller, 2000, p. 17). Moreover, the phallic figure that becomes the woman beckons the primary question for being: "Am I a man or a woman?" Freudian and Lacanian approaches suggest that a common trait of the hysteric is to return to this question in an attempt to define one's identity, which can only be attempted in relation to the Other (Fink, 2009, p. 122).

Like Dorothy Vallens, The Girl's trauma is manifested in the body, which then acts as a site for the collision of two contradictory human qualities: On the one hand, there is innocence and vulnerability; and on the other, destruction. For The Girl, destruction is represented by the spewing of blood upon the white sheets, symbolising a violation of purity.

Cases: Laura Palmer and Thanatos

Freud believed that humans had a life drive (Eros) which includes love, creativity, sexuality, production, and the ambition for reproduction. Its counterpart, the death drive (Thanatos), is also inherent, and conversely supplies us with the inclination for destruction and aggression. As we have seen so far, the Lynchian hysteric is characterised by her tendencies toward the death drive, and the destructive trait is most notably directed at herself.

The hysteric materialises in a seminal character from Lynch's oeuvre: Laura Palmer. Laura Palmer's death is the catapulting event from which the cult series *Twin Peaks* (1990–1991) emerges and is the subject of the prequel film *Twin Peaks: Fire Walk With Me* (1992). The first season of *Twin Peaks* opens on her murder as she is found wrapped in plastic, and follows an FBI investigation that objectively traces the possible routes that lead to her death.

The audience initially learns that Laura was a generous, young woman with great popularity, who selflessly volunteered and contributed to her community. She was a bright student at school and had a part-time job at a department store. However, the first series of *Twin Peaks* unearths that she was addicted to cocaine, worked as a prostitute at a casino called One Eyed Jack's, and had a plethora of relationships with men who loved her but for whom she felt nothing. The root cause of her behaviour appears to arise from years of sexual abuse at the hands of her father, Leland Palmer (Ray Wise), as he was possessed by an evil force named BOB (Frank Silva).

The scene of Laura's trauma is revealed in *Fire Walk With Me.* It begins as a similar scenario seen in *The Alphabet*: A young woman innocently lies asleep in her bed covered in clean white sheets. Soon appears the figure of BOB climbing in through the window, crawling into bed with her, and raping her. Laura asks the man on top of her who he is. Upon finally addressing the perpetrator whom she has seen on several occasions, she no longer sees the face of BOB but Leland Palmer, her father; Laura's scream sends shockwaves. Her behaviour to cope with the trauma is also explored in the series as she develops self-destructive tendencies. The Freudian death drive rears its ugly head once again in her cocaine habit and her desire for several sexual pursuits at once. She persistently seeks a satisfaction that can't be fulfilled.

Like Dorothy Vallens in *Blue Velvet*, we witness the collapse of Laura's fantasy into reality. Sexual abuse by her father had been masked by a desire for it to be anyone else, by the fictional face of BOB, by her other relationships, by her clients as a call girl at the casino (including her father's business partner, Ben Horne). Like Dorothy, Laura's body is a site for corruption and a conflicting figure. Eventually, she is removed altogether.

We only have to look as far as Ronette Pulanski (Phoebe Augustine), who is found wandering over a bridge wearing nothing but a ripped white fabric, to discover the reality of Laura's trauma. Although not a main character, Ronette appears in the pilot episode of *Twin Peaks*. She is found by a lumberjack staggering out of the woods. She is severely injured and cannot speak. Once brought to a hospital, the doctor informs Agent Cooper (Kyle MacLachlan) that she has been raped multiple times and has possibly suffered neurological damage. This is a similar vision to Dorothy Vallens appearing in the street outside Jeffrey's house.

Cases: Audrey Horne and Freud's Dora

The *Twin Peaks* character Audrey Horne (Sherilyn Fenn) is often seen as the sultry dark-haired parallel of the ill-fated Laura Palmer. Laura is the admirable, blonde, bright-eyed Homecoming Queen; meanwhile, Audrey is rich, superficial, and mostly overlooked by the other characters of the series, especially her own father.

Like Laura, Audrey has her own dual personality. First impressions make her appear cunning, callous (pretending to be saddened by Laura's death), and overtly full of desire; contrarily, she is affectionate, thoughtful, and longs for love. Her infatuation for the protagonist Agent Cooper made her one of the audience's favourite characters of the whole series. Audrey Horne most notably desired the affection and attention of her father, Ben Horne (Richard Beymer), a wealthy business magnate in Twin Peaks, who hardly ever prescribed her this type of love. The relationship between Ben and Audrey is integral for understanding her status as a Lynchian hysteric.

The father–daughter dynamic is a prevalent trope of one of Sigmund Freud's most famous case studies, Dora (the pseudonym of his patient, Ida Bauer). She came to him in 1900 for treatment, as she was suffering serious bouts of acute aphonia (the inability to speak), a distinct symptom of hysteria. Freud called the publication of this case *Fragment of Analysis of a Case of Hysteria* (1905e), as she terminated her analysis after only eleven weeks.

What transpired in Freud's sessions with Dora is that she had learned that her father was having an extra-marital affair with a woman known as Frau K. Frau K's husband—Herr K—was a close companion of her father. Because of her knowledge, Dora became a confidante for both Frau K and her father, keeping it from their respective partners, including her mother. Her mother is only mentioned in the publication briefly as a "foolish, uncultivated woman" who had "housewife's psychosis", being obsessed with cleanliness (Freud, 1905e, p. 19). Meanwhile, Dora described her father as the more "dominant" character (Freud, 1905e, p. 17), frequently analysing how she could fit herself into his life.

Audrey Horne also discovers her father's extra-marital affair with a woman called Catherine Martell (Piper Laurie). Much like Jeffrey Beaumont in *Blue Velvet*, she watches them secretly converse and kiss from a hole in a hidden closet looking into her father's office. She appears transfixed with the scene unfolding before her eyes. Like Dora, Audrey's mother is hardly a featured character in the first two seasons of *Twin Peaks*. She is far more preoccupied with her father, whose story she is still piecing together.

In Dora's case, she had been spending an increasing amount of time with Herr K. He was attracted to her and had set out to seduce her when she was still of a young age, bringing her flowers and gifts. When Dora was 14 years old, Herr K had made an attempt to kiss her, and three years later tried to seduce her, but she slapped him in the face and hurried away. Dora told her mother of the incident, but Herr K, Frau K, and her father claimed that all of this was a fantasy of her own desires. This is when her symptoms surfaced. Freud let her know that he believed her account but deduced that she did have repressed, unconscious desire for Herr K as well as for her father. Freud also believed that she was repressing homosexual desire for Frau K too. Dora met this analysis with disdain, and this was the moment she left therapy with Freud.

Comparatively, Audrey was attracted to Agent Cooper from the start, curious about his life and assisting him with his investigations. As a career-driven older man, he is the ideal character for Audrey to transfer her repressed feelings for her father. Upon finding out about her father's affair with Catherine, Audrey is driven to actively pursue Agent Cooper. He finds her in his bed waiting for him to return to his room, trying to seduce him. She sought the attention of her father; she sought the attention of Agent Cooper, both to no avail. Her efforts had been rejected.

Whilst Dora harboured feelings for Frau K, Audrey also harboured feelings for Laura Palmer. She sees something of herself in Laura, whom she later finds out had sexual relations with her father at One Eyed Jack's. She identifies her affection for Laura by stating that they were not really friends but that she had "kind of loved Laura". Laura symbolised someone that Audrey wanted to be, the object of men's fantasies: the subject of Agent Cooper's investigations and someone whom her father desired.

Twenty-five years later, *Twin Peaks: The Return* (2017) marks the height of Audrey's hysteria. The first two seasons of *Twin Peaks* sketch out her teenage experiences and traumas. She even risks her life at One Eyed Jack's for Agent Cooper's investigation, but this is less martyrdom and more naivety. One of her final moments at One Eyed Jack's allows Audrey to have a taste of what it is like to be wanted by her father as she goes undercover as a call girl, putting herself in the place of Laura Palmer. She is masked so he does not recognise her and tries to have sex with her. She cannot face it and tries to evade him, but this extends his longing. The passion only diffuses when there is a knock at the door.

Audrey faces the convergence of reality and fantasy again when *Twin Peaks* comes to a surreal end in *Twin Peaks: The Return*. Agent Cooper is replaced with Mr C ("Evil Cooper") and it is unearthed that he raped her, leaving her pregnant with their son known as Richard Horne (Eamon Farron). This great trauma that occurs at the hands of Evil Cooper sends her into what we can only deduce is a breakdown as she is generally absent from the whole series. We suspect that she is comatose and stuck in a vegetative state, or institutionalised, as she is seen wearing all white in a white room—iconographic of a sanatorium. She appears to be imagining delusional scenes of a relationship between her and her therapist. This transference is also present in Dora's case. Freud noted in his posthumous analysis that Dora had misdirected feelings for Herr K—and her father—onto the psychoanalyst, Sigmund Freud himself (Freud, 1905e, p. 115).

Both narratives are incomplete, fragmented, when their stories are cut short. This time, we (the reader, the spectator, the audience) are left desiring more from her, hoping that she will complete the story. So who's the hysterical one now?

Hystericising the audience

The specific tropes of the Lynchian hysteric coincide somewhat with the psychoanalytic models of hysteria. Firstly, she has masochistic tendencies, and there tends to be an indication of sexual trauma. These are common traits found in Freud's case studies. Lynch plays with boundaries and stereotypes of "femininity" in his hysterical characters: mother, young woman, virgin, whore. She does not fit neatly into any of these categories; she frightens, shocks, and is constantly defying expectations. She initiates longing from the audience, and her mystery permits us to project our own desires onto her.

Secondly, Lynch has drawn upon classical depictions of hysteria, as the hysteric is always in the body of the Woman—the Other—that the protagonists and spectators alike cannot figure out. The Lynchian hysteric is not just "the other" gender but also the product of two worlds colliding: an "ideal" world coming into contact with a netherworld, a world of doppelgängers, a world of the uncanny. Lynch makes her a mysterious character not for us to fully comprehend. She falls somewhere between the object of male fantasy and the perpetrator of her own masochistic desires.

References

Feiner, K. & Knafo, D. (2002). *Blue Velvet*: David Lynch's Primal Scene. *International Journal of Psycho-Analysis* 83(6): 1445–1451.

Fink, B. (2009). *A Clinical Introduction to Lacanian Psychoanalysis: Theory and Technique*. Cambridge: Harvard University Press.

Freud, S. & Breuer, J. (1895d). *Studies on Hysteria. S. E.*, 2. London: Hogarth.

Freud, S. (1905e). *Fragment of an Analysis of a Case of Hysteria. S. E.*, 7. London: Hogarth.

Gessert, A. (2014). *Introductory Lectures on Lacan*. London: Karnac.

Hustvedt, A. (2011). *Medical Muses: Hysteria in 19th Century Paris*. New York, NY: W. W. Norton.

Jones, E. (1955). *Sigmund Freud: Life and Work. Volume II: Years of Maturity, 1901–1919*. London: Hogarth.

McGowan, T. (2007). *The Impossible David Lynch*. New York, NY: Columbia University Press.

Miller, J-A. (2000). The Relation Between the Sexes. In: Salecl, R. (Ed.) *Sexuation*. Durham and London: Duke University Press.

Mulvey, L. (1996). *Fetishism and Curiosity: The Mind's Eye*. Bloomington, IN: Indiana University Press.

Rodley, C. (2005). *Lynch on Lynch (Revised Edition)*. London: Faber & Faber.

CHAPTER 7

Möbian adventures on the lost highway

Stefan Marianski

> As soon as he wishes to speak, man is oriented in the fundamental topology of language.
>
> (Lacan, 1977, p. 244)

"Dick Laurent is dead". So goes the enigmatic sentence that both opens and closes David Lynch's 1997 masterpiece *Lost Highway*. A signifier that both opens and closes is an interesting notion in itself, enacting the simultaneous rupture and continuity that paradoxically characterises the function of the "cut" in Lacanian psychoanalysis: the cut of the signifier that constitutes the subject, effecting a subtraction of its causal object (evidently an invocatory object for the film's Janus-faced antihero with the "best goddamn ears in town"). Isolated by the cut, this is the object that falls away in the moments that follow: in the screech of tyres and the police siren that fades as Fred Madison (Bill Pullman) scrambles to the window, whereupon it functions in the fantasy as the cause of desire. A key tenet of Lacanian psychoanalysis is that it is only through an operation of subtraction that the field of reality holds together, such that a few short seconds later Fred can peer out of the window of 7035

Hollis (near the observatory) and see … nothing. Fantasy, as Lacan fittingly puts it in *Seminar X*, is "about *not* seeing what stands to be beheld outside the window" (2014, p. 73).

In what sense does "Dick Laurent is dead" instate the cut of the signifier? Precisely in the sense that it is not identical to itself. Despite being one and the same utterance, *the line that closes the film is strictly non-equivalent to the one that opens it*. The following comments are guided by an insistence on this paradoxical non-equivalence, not as a paradox that must be resolved but rather as one that determines the structure of the film as a surface. My contention is that the structure of *Lost Highway* can be investigated through Lacanian topology, and I sketch out some preliminary contours of such an investigation in what follows.

The repetition of "Dick Laurent is dead" puts us on the trail of the repetition of the "unary trait", a concept Lacan extracts from Freud's work in order to conceptualise the first encounter with language, an encounter that must be qualified as traumatic in that the effect it produces is not in the first instance one of meaning but of jouissance. That is to say, of an excitation that cannot be mastered, prompting its compulsive repetition in the manner described by Freud in *Beyond the Pleasure Principle* (1920g). Indeed, it is the *repetition* of the trait that constitutes the barred subject proper: the trait is a signifier and thus a unit of difference, requiring a second inscription to retroactively allow the first to count as one. This second inscription, however, retains the differential property of the signifier—what Lacan in *Seminar IX* refers to as the signifier's "fecundity"—which extends to its own self-difference:

> From this fact, that [the signifier] cannot be defined except precisely by not being all the other signifiers, on this there depends this dimension that it is equally true that it cannot be itself.
>
> (1961–1962, p. 31)

In other words, the second inscription of the signifier cannot be understood to be an identical reproduction of the first. The fecundity of the signifier means that there can be no self-identity in language, that "there is no tautology" (loc. cit.), a statement that surely belongs in the pantheon of Lacanian aphorisms (the Lynchian equivalent of which might be said to run: "the owls are not what they seem"). The repetition entails a failure of tautology which can be written as $a \neq a$, casting the subject of its address into the gap it generates:

> There is necessarily produced somewhere, from the fact that the signifier redoubles itself, is summoned to the function of signifying itself, a field which is one of exclusion and through which the subject is rejected into the outside field.
>
> (Lacan, 1961–1962, p. 216)

Yet the field of exclusion to which the subject is banished is not an outside. It is, as Lacan would later elaborate, an exclusion *internal* to the structure of the signifier, the place of an impossible real located not beyond language but *folded into its very structure*. This field of internal exclusion shows itself in the path traced by this elementary repetition: rather than returning directly back to a self-identical starting point (Figure 1), its trajectory, in Greenshields' words, "adds an extra loop ($a \neq a$) to the circle's tautology ($a = a$)" (Greenshields, 2017, p. 43), constituting the topological figure of the interior eight (Figure 2). In their non-equivalence, the two instances of the same utterance "Dick Laurent is dead" support the elaboration of a topology. The signifier's path is a strange and difficult one.

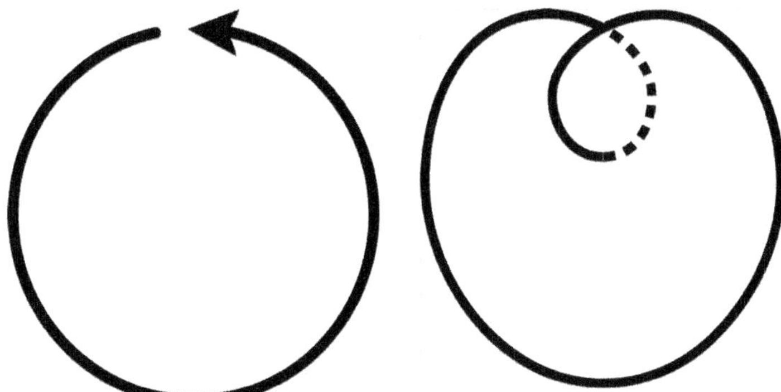

Figures 1 and 2: tautological loop and interior eight

The extra loop of $a \neq a$ thus marks out the place of the internally excluded real of the signifying economy, a structural fault around which significations can crystallise, but which cannot be mastered via the network of signifiers, neither by painstaking structural analysis nor by years on the couch. It is a point of unthinkability that haunts the signifying chain. While it gives our symbolic reality its particular form, it cannot be grasped or anticipated from within it: the intrusion of the real is thus always a chance encounter, a contingency, something that disturbs the continuity of our experience of reality, and which our first inclination is to cover over. An absolute fidelity to such chance encounters is characteristic of Lynch's singular filmmaking ethic. Indeed, we might even go so far as to say that this is what marks his creative process as Cartesian, in the sense that Lacan (1977) qualifies Freud's method as Cartesian: when there appears a thought so incongruous, so unlikely, so foreign to our understanding that our first inclination is to doubt its value, that is where Lynch, like Freud, affirms the certainty of a clear and distinct idea.

The signifying operation that generates this topology is also what causes the subject to disappear at the very moment of its constitution in the field of the Other, the signifier that would represent the subject for all the other signifiers being always already excluded from the signifying network. This is why Lacan maintains that the subject of the unconscious is ultimately nameless (Lacan, 2006, p. 700), and perhaps this supplies a preliminary clue to the function of the Mystery Man (Robert Blake), who asks Fred "What the fuck is your name?!" Indeed, if Lacan articulates a subject that disappears at the moment of its constitution, we would do well to note that such disappearances are a staple of Lynch's cinematic *oeuvre*, the most sustained exposition of which is undoubtedly Dale Cooper's (Kyle MacLachlan) peculiar absence from the text of *Twin Peaks: The Return* (2017), peculiar because it is not really an absence at all: the Arm's Doppelgänger's cry of "non-exist-ent!" as Cooper is evacuated from the Black Lodge does not mark the revocation of a previously held ontological status; it installs him in the fold of the signifier, the point of a rupture in Being that reverberates through the symbolic fabric of the series.

In this sense, Lynch shares with Lacan what has come to be referred to as a "negative ontology": where we expect to find something essential about Being, we instead encounter a gap (albeit one with a structuring function). This negativity is just as much at stake in the Mystery Man's "What the fuck is your name?!" as it is in the question that haunts

The Return, Monica Bellucci's "Who [the fuck] is the dreamer?!" Moreover, it will come as no surprise to Lacanian viewers of *The Return* that, prior to coming to inhabit the body of Dougie Jones, Cooper first passes through the glass box, the site of a violent disruption of a sexual encounter. As we will see below, this point of a rupture in Being is closely tied to what Lacan describes as the absence of the sexual relationship, an impossibility that the cut of the signifier inscribes on the body.

A place both wonderful and strange

The field of internal exclusion established by the repetition of "Dick Laurent is dead" is what renders the structure of *Lost Highway* Möbian, the interior eight constituting—in Lacan's "*topologerie*" (Nasio, 2004, p. 102)—the single edge of the Möbius strip (Figure 3), that confounding topological surface to which Lynch compared the film (Henry, 1997) and to which Lacan claimed the subject of the unconscious is structurally equivalent. In the later years of his work, Lacan became increasingly preoccupied with topology, the so-called "rubber geometry" whose surfaces retain invariant qualities, irrespective of distortion or stretching.

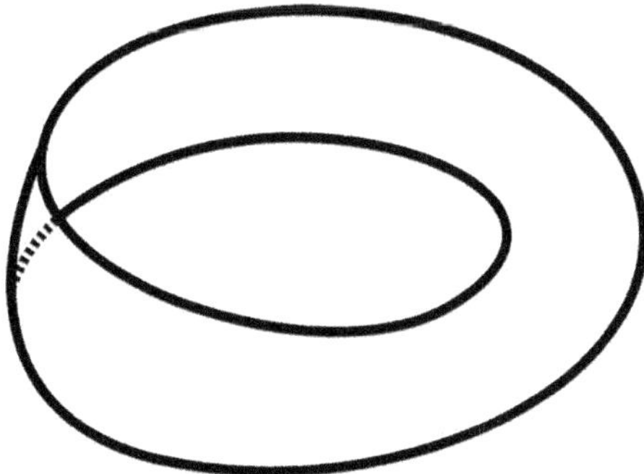

Figure 3: Möbius strip

What qualifies *Lost Highway* as Möbian is not merely the trajectory of its narrative arc. It is not that the plot traces the shape of a Möbius strip as intuitively represented in ordinary Euclidian space, curving around to the left before passing under itself, veering around to the right, etc. Fred is not figuratively driving along the Möbius strip, tracing its highways and byways in Mr Eddy's (Robert Loggia) Mercedes-Benz

450SEL (aptly specified in the screenplay as a "Pullman" model). While topology captures a fundamentally spatio-*temporal* logic, a topological reading of *Lost Highway* must to some extent suspend the temptation to glibly map the film's storyline as it unfolds chronologically onto the surface in question. The Möbius strip is non-orientable, resisting our habitual recourse to notions of left and right, top and bottom, or inside and outside in our attempts to designate a path on its surface. Its length or width are similarly irrelevant to the topology of surfaces, which is concerned solely with structural qualities that remain invariant throughout continuous deformation.

Locally, the Möbius strip might appear to have two sides (just as *Lost Highway* appears to have two complementary storylines), but globally it turns out to have only one: a hypothetical line drawn along its surface will pass seamlessly over to what our feeble intuition takes to be its "other side" before passing seamlessly again to its point of departure. Crucially, the exact location of the twist that defines it as a surface cannot be established in a topological space. As Stone puts it:

> [T]he Möbius strip is defined not in terms of any fixed locus or loci but by a twist displaceable throughout its length [...] We cannot pinpoint this twist in any definitive manner without the surface or line losing its Möbian nature. The twist, thus, is the real of the Möbius strip.
>
> (Stone, 1998, quoted in Greenshields, 2017, p. 48)

Insofar as *Lost Highway* is Möbian, it is not a matter of pinpointing the twist, of locating it at, say, the moment of Fred's transformation into Pete. Even if we could, we would then be obliged to admit a second twist when Pete transforms back into Fred, and the Möbian structure would be lost (to constitute a Möbius strip, the number of twists must be odd). Commenting on the elusive twist, Greenshields (2017) notes that it is

> not simply absent from the structure for it has made the structure what it is. While it is, strictly speaking, nowhere (it being unlocalisable), its effects are discernable everywhere—it is, to use one of Lacan's neologisms "nullibiquitous".
>
> (Greenshields, 2017, p. 49)

Rather than corresponding to the narrative technique of the "plot twist", what bears witness to this nullibiquitous twist *qua* real is its effects on the filmic text. The twist supports a hole which, unlike the (false) hole one obtains by tracing a circle—the tautological loop $a=a$ of Figure 1—is *irreducible*: it cannot be closed.

Lacan's notion of an irreducible hole in the signifying structure is in keeping with his reformulation of the theory of "primal repression", the concept by means of which Freud (1915d) sought to account for the fact that, in order for repression proper to operate, there must already be a pre-existing unconscious locus to which subsequently repressed ideas can be bound. Lacan's treatment of the problem foregrounds what we have identified as the irreducible Möbian hole: that the imposition of language comes not as a fully articulable and ordered totality, but rather as including within it the very impossibility of its totalisation. The hole *qua* primal repression is thus the incompleteness of the signifying apparatus. As Zupančič rather more eloquently puts it, "the signifying order emerges as already lacking one signifier [...] it appears with the lack of a signifier 'built into it', so to speak" (Zupančič, 2017, p. 42). If what Freud identified as primal repression turns out not to be a piece of repressed content but a structural fault in language that "ensures the incompletion of every meaning effect" (Greenshields, 2017, p. 93), we can already sketch out a key interpretative precept that our topology demands: interpretation should not seek to fill the hole, but to examine how the film negotiates the inherent impossibility that gives it its unique structure. With this in mind, let us turn to *Lost Highway*.

One meaning less

Characterised by Herzogenrath as "a disturbing study of contemporary marital hell" (Herzogenrath, 1999), the ominous first part of *Lost Highway* can be divided into three sequences. Each sequence includes at its apex a bedroom scene, diegetically marked by Lynch's trademark red curtains, and each closes with the arrival of a videotape. The first sequence begins with an exchange between Fred and his wife Renee (Patricia Arquette). In this crucial dialogue, the first in the film (apart from the enigmatic message "Dick Laurent is dead"), we get a glimpse of the Madisons' domestic life together and immediately discern that something isn't quite right:

RENEE: You don't mind that I'm not coming to the club tonight?
FRED: What are you going to do?
RENEE: Stay home, read.
FRED: Read? Read what, Renee?
RENEE: (laughs)
FRED: It's nice to know I can still make you laugh
RENEE: I like to laugh, Fred.
FRED: That's why I married you.
RENEE: You can wake me up when you get home if you want to.

Recalling our filmic topology, we should be on our guard against speciously filling the hole our Möbian structure organises with vague personality traits. Lacan's topological rigour is strictly opposed to such "inexact, synthesising concepts such as personality—products of misleading ego identifications which clog the analytic session with self-regarding waffle ('I'm the kind of person who …')" (Greenshields, 2017, p. 41). A psychoanalytic reading is not content to say merely that Fred is "the kind of person who has jealous tendencies" or that Renee is "the kind of person who shuts men out". Even when such readings situate their purported traits as repressed ("Fred is unconsciously jealous", etc.), the question of repressed *content* is a red herring that invariably "clogs" the Möbian hole as a structural fault in language. Such readings seek to shore up its defining tautological failure through the introduction of a metalanguage that ultimately can only serve to accentuate the unfathomable gap from which arises the dimension of the unconscious (ibid. p. 29).

Fred (Bill Pullman) and Renee (Patricia Arquette) in *Lost Highway* (1997), dir. Lynch, courtesy of BFI Stills, Posters and Designs

What if, rather than mobilising character traits in an attempt to formulate Fred and Renee's relationship, we instead approached their exchanges from the perspective discussed above, that of a failure pertaining to language itself? Chion points the way to this reading with the following astute observation: rather than resolving itself into a meaning, the staging of Fred and Renee's opening exchange instead produces a gap, an *absence* of meaning. "Instead of the implication we might expect", he writes, Lynch "adds precisely nothing at all [...] it has what might be called *one meaning less*" (Chion, 2006, p. 195, emphasis added). Reading Chion with Lacan, we can note that what is at stake here is not an element of meaning that has been excluded from the symbolic fabric of the film but an element of meaninglessness that has been *included* in it: the "one meaning less" is strictly correlative with the irreducible hole that our Möbian twist sustains, the effect of which, as McGowan notes, is that no answer Renee could give would be satisfactory to Fred (McGowan, 2007, p. 159). The interpretative task is not to recover a purportedly missing element so as to restore what we imagine to be a prior state of ordered totality—in Lacanese, this is the erroneous hermeneutical endeavour of clogging the Möbian hole by placing $-\varphi$ in the place of S(Ⱥ)—but rather to trace how this element of meaninglessness "has important consequences for the field structured around it" (Zupančič, 2017, p. 22).

It's not working out

If *Lost Highway* negotiates an inherent fault in the signifying order, it also shows that the element of meaninglessness this fault engenders pertains specifically to relations between sexed beings: our liaisons have to negotiate this logical impasse that led Lacan to proclaim "there is no sexual relationship". The pithiness of Lacan's aphorism belies the rigorous formalisation that accompanies its elaboration in *Seminar XX*, yet he also maintains that it is an obvious and readily observable fact of human experience: "What constitutes the basis of life, in effect, is that for everything having to do with relations between men and women [...] it's not working out" (Lacan, 1999, p. 32). Like the nullibiquitous Möbian twist, the sexual relationship is an impossibility that "does not stop not being written" (Lacan, 1999, p. 144). It is what gives rise to the everyday problems of our love and sex misadventures, which on closer inspection turn out not to be manifestations of the impossibility but attempts at solutions. The sexual non-relationship is thus consonant with our topology, constituting a hole in discursive space, revealing the latter to be "generated out of, and around, a missing link in the ontological chain of its own reality" (Zupančič, 2017, p. 24).

While most clearly evident in the oft-discussed sex scene and the anxiety dream it provokes Fred to tell Renee about, the consequences of the sexual non-relationship run through the entirety of the first part of the film, not only in the three bedroom encounters—all of which, of course, turn out to be non-encounters—but also in the business of the videotapes that arrive immediately after each of them. Indeed, these black, rectangular objects that intrude forebodingly into the Madisons' reality with such calamitous effects are vaguely evocative of the monoliths of Stanley Kubrick's *2001: A Space Odyssey* (1968) which, as Bristow comments in his magisterial study of the film, can be read as materialising the inaugural cut of the subject (Bristow, 2017). Significantly, when the arrival of the second videotape provokes a distraught Renee to call the police, she tells them that someone has taped the couple … sleeping. "Isn't that enough?!" she adds, which is, like much of the film's dialogue, an equivocal statement, testifying to the slippage and fragmentation that language undergoes in the proximity of the hole that the sexual non-relationship constitutes.

Lynchian detectives

If the videotapes mark "a certain non-rapport between the couple", as Dravers writes of *The Purloined Letter* (1844) in Edgar Allen Poe's eponymous story (Dravers, 2004, p. 209), they also occasion the involvement of the decidedly un-Dupinian detectives Ed (Lou Eppolito) and Al (John Roselius). "That's it", Fred, in another equivocal statement, tells our monosyllabic snoops when the tape of the sleeping couple ends. The detectives are especially interested in the sleeping arrangement. "You sleep here?" Al asks, "In this room? Both of yous?" and in an awkward exchange, Fred is forced to admit that there is in fact another bedroom ("I use it as a practice room"). Commenting on the scene, Santini remarks that it is as though the detectives suspect that Fred's true crime is his inability to satisfy his wife sexually (Santini, 2017). If this is the case—if they truly suspect him of being "the kind of person who can't satisfy Renee", indeed the kind who might murder her in a fit of impotent rage—it would mark them as dupes of the characterological red herring discussed above. Pushing the idea a little further, we might even say that Ed and Al suffer from the same dimensional impairment that Lacan decries in the police of *The Purloined Letter* as "the imbecility of the realist" (Lacan, 2006, p. 17). While admittedly lacking the geometric precision with which the police of Poe's tale search the Minister's apartment, Ed and Al's poke around the Madisons' house nonetheless demonstrates a similar failure to properly comprehend the topology of the surface on which their search takes place. Checking the windows and doors to "see if anybody tried to break in" comes across as more than a little absurd given the ways of the Mystery Man and the nullibiquitous openings by means of which he finds his invitation, that is, from a Lacanian perspective, through Fred's retreat from the ethical question of his responsibility before the elusive real of the sexual non-rapport. It is for this reason that the Mystery Man incarnates the true face of the superego, as McGowan has also observed (McGowan, 2007, p. 162).

The detectives, by contrast, might be on the trail of Fred's implicatedness in the structural fault but nonetheless remain blind to it. Despite entering the film in the aftermath of the appearance of the real within its structure, their apparent working assumption that Fred is *hiding something* is an assumption that effaces the real, making it a police matter, thus demonstrating their "fidelity to the elementary topology that marks out their area of jurisdiction, namely reality insofar as it is framed by the fantasy", as Dravers writes of the police of Poe's tale (Dravers, 2004, p. 211). No wonder the screenplay has them exchanging notes on the impossibly high camera angle of the videotape (Lynch & Gifford, 1997, p. 17), a bafflement we also observe in the prison wardens' discovery of the impossible disappearance of Fred from his jail cell and his replacement by Pete Dayton (Balthazar Getty), obliging them to announce in a press conference (in the screenplay) what they can only comprehend as Fred's escape. Such is how fantasy treats the impossible real, making Ed and Al's sleuthing a far cry from that of, say, Dale Cooper in *Twin Peaks* (1990–1991) or Jeffrey Beaumont in *Blue Velvet* (1986). Moreover, Ed and Al's imbecilic realism is also an imbecilic moralism: through the frame of fantasy, the properly *ethical* question of Fred's responsibility as a sexed being can only register in its effects as a *moral* one pertaining to his conduct with Renee.

Who the hell owns that dog?

Much has been made of the centrality of desire to *Lost Highway*. In his masterly study, McGowan makes a compelling case for reading the film's two parts as depicting respective worlds of desire and fantasy (McGowan, 2007). Lynch's genius, in McGowan's reading, is to hold apart what in everyday experience are for the most part indissolubly linked, and, in doing so, revealing how fantasy sustains the experience of reality by giving the desire of the Other a minimal consistency. A slightly nuanced perspective, corresponding to a shift in Lacan's conceptualisation of desire that occurs in the mid-1960s, would be to treat the first part not as depicting a "world of pure desire" (ibid. p. 157), independent of and somehow anterior to its fantasy frame, but rather a world in which fantasy is operative, albeit haphazardly so, sustaining reality by producing and orienting the desire of the Other, so that its real causal object is—save for certain moments—veiled. In this perspective, it is only insofar as object *a* is framed in the fantasy that it can function as the truth of desire, which in Lacanian psychoanalysis is always a fictive and partial truth, to be carefully differentiated from the real.

What indicates that fantasy is operative in the first part of the film? We began by noting that the opening scene stages the cut of the signifier and the fall of the object. That Fred sees *nothing* by the time he gets to the window suggests that the intrusion of "Dick Laurent is dead" is immediately followed by a subtraction, and even the window itself evokes the fantasy, constituting a frame through which one looks in order not to see something. A similar fantasmatic elision could be said to be operative for Fred to ask "who the hell owns that dog?" the morning after his failed sexual encounter with Renee—a line which never fails to provoke a titter among cinema audiences—an obvious dysphemism for "what the hell causes Renee's desire?". The very phrasing of Fred's question already provides a minimal frame: "that dog" answers to someone, and this is also what we glimpse in Fred's image of Renee leaving the Luna Lounge with Andy.

We also noted earlier that the privileged form of object *a* in the film is the invocatory object, that is, an object pertaining to the dimension of the voice. This is indicated in Fred/Pete's astute hearing, but also in Renee's breath: her almost inconspicuous sighs and gasps, especially when the videotapes are in close proximity. Not traditionally considered to be a face of the object-voice in Lacanian psychoanalysis, the filmic cut lends the breath its status, most noticeably during Renee's phone call to the police, the close-up isolating her mouth, and the sound accentuating her sigh just before she speaks, foregrounding that an object has come to the place of what remains indecipherable in the Other. "There are things you can't get anywhere", *Twin Peaks*' Harold Smith (Lenny Von Dohlen) astutely puts it, "but we dream they can be found in other people".

The fantasy thus concerns the articulation of two "pieces" established by the cut of the signifier: the subject as constitutively barred and the object as constitutively lost, hence Lacan's formula of fantasy, $\$\lozenge a$. Happily, this has a precise topological articulation: recalling once more the Möbian topology of the subject, fantasy concerns the grafting of a bilateral disc onto the edge of a Möbius strip, which is also the edge of the latter's irreducible hole. The topological surface thus produced is what Lacan called a cross-cap (Figure 4)—although mathematicians would call it a sphere equipped with a cross-cap—which the cut of the interior eight can separate *vice versa* into a Möbius strip and a disc.

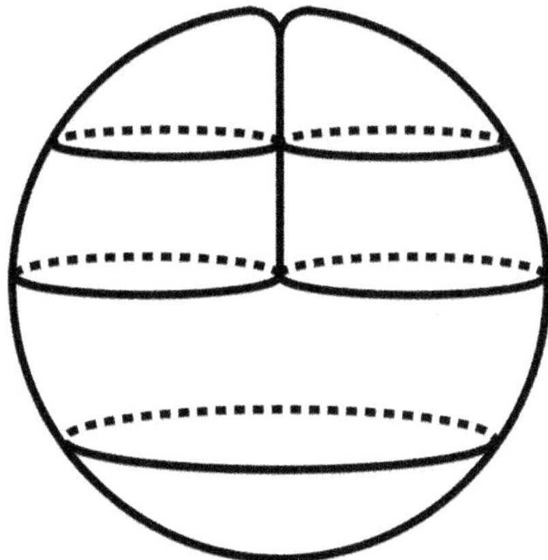

Figure 4: Immersion of a cross-capped sphere. The upper portion is homeomorphic to a Möbius strip; and the lower portion, to a disc

The cross-cap has a number of remarkable qualities. In contrast to the Möbius strip it does not have an edge, although it preserves the Möbian quality of inside and outside being in continuity: a line traced around what appears to be its outside will pass over to its apparent inside, which becomes even more surprising when we realise that the line of self-intersection where the flip appears to occur does not mathematically exist, only appearing in Figure 4 due to the dimensional limitations of the immersion. But perhaps the most unsettling of its features is that, despite the fact that one can obtain the surface by grafting a disc onto the edge of a Möbius strip, the closing of the surface does not eliminate the Möbian hole. The cross-cap retains, if not strictly speaking a hole, an "unimaginable point at its centre" (Lafont, 1986, p. 42) to which the Möbian hole has been reduced, without being closed. This unimaginable point is all the more striking when we learn that the surface is topologically equivalent to the real projective plane with its vanishing point at infinity.

Transposing this peculiarity back into the psychoanalytic register of fantasy, we can see why fantasy does not simply stage the recovery of the constitutively lost object. The temptation to be avoided is to read the second part of the film as enacting the clichéd "escape from reality" to a world in which the satisfaction missing from ordinary life is recovered. Even the younger and more virile Pete Dayton, although commencing a passionate affair with Alice Wakefield (also played by Patricia Arquette), ultimately doesn't get the girl; on the contrary, his involvement with Alice is what causes reality to splinter and collapse. The second part of the film discloses the fantasy frame that invisibly structures the first, so that what we witness is the crossing of the screen of fantasy, resulting not in the revelation of an unbearable truth but instead in the provoking of an impossible real over which the object *a* was placed as semblant.

Rather than plugging the Möbian hole, what fantasy stages is the cut from which it derives its structure (Lacan, 2006, p. 486); the cut that simultaneously separates and connects the barred subject and the object *a*; the cut to which subsequent disturbances in the field of reality can be indexed with the help of the phallic function. Thus, it is not about fulfilling wishes or making the impossible possible, least of all the impossibility of the sexual relationship, despite being "the only recourse the subject has in the face of the sexual non-relation" (Morel, 2019,

p. 39). Rather, it involves a reshuffling of the elements of reality so as to give the impossibility a signifying frame. If sexuality is "the result of an attempt to invent a logic at the very point of impasse of such logic" (Zupančič, 2017, p. 43), the fantasy is the scene of this invention. In the second part of *Lost Highway*, we thus enter into the phallic logic by which man—the film dwells extensively on the typically *male* mode of navigating this impasse—attempts to patch up the sexual non-relation by making it a matter of castration. The logic at play is the one we find written on the masculine side of Lacan's famous formulas of sexuation. The first part of the formula, written as $\forall x\ \Phi x$, posits the universality of castration: all speaking beings ($\forall x$) are submitted to the phallic function (Φx), while the second part, written as $\exists x\ \neg\Phi x$, shows that the universality of the phallic function is grounded by an exception: there exists a speaking being ($\exists x$) that is not submitted to the phallic function ($\neg\Phi x$), whose jouissance is not subject to a limit, the primal father of Freud's *Totem and Taboo* (1912–1913), both beyond the law of castration and the necessary condition for its possibility.

Why are there people like Frank?

In mobilising a phallic logic, the fantasy foregrounds the exception to the law of castration, incarnated by the figure of Mr Eddy, the ruthless gangster who monopolises Alice, and who is also excessively preoccupied with upholding traffic laws. Indeed, Mr Eddy is an instance of an ongoing preoccupation in Lynch's filmic worlds with menacing, transgressive father figures policing relatively banal rules, from *Dune*'s (1984) Baron Harkonnen (Kenneth McMillan) admonishing the moribund Duke Leto (Jürgen Prochnow) for his "carelessness" and *Blue Velvet*'s Frank Booth (Dennis Hopper) screaming at Jeffrey Beaumont (Kyle MacLachlan) to "be polite!" to Leland Palmer (Ray Wise) in the chilling "Laura didn't wash her hands before dinner" scene in *Twin Peaks: Fire Walk With Me* (1992). As phallic exception, Mr Eddy testifies to how the fantasy injects circumstance into the facticity of loss. It is through his interdiction that an obstacle *inherent* to sexuality, unavoidably produced by a structural fault in language, can be framed as an *external* one, as Žižek (2000) and McGowan (2007) have both noted, so that what is constitutively missing can be registered as something of which we have been deprived. In Zupančič's words:

> Everyone has to give up on what they never had—*yet the form of giving it up is nonetheless essential.* This is perhaps also the best definition of castration: to give up on what one never had, that is to say, to transform what we never had into something lost.
>
> (Zupančič, 2017, p. 51)

Rather than being the radical edge of human subjectivity announced by Freud, with Lacan the law of castration thus turns out to be a secondary elaboration, a mask for a more fundamental discordance. We can no longer be content to say that the law generates desire by prohibiting its object; it is rather that the very structuring of desire through its conjugation with the law veils the true state of affairs, the irremediable incompleteness of the Other of language that leaves it exposed to the real. While in some sense each point of enigma in the first part of the film finds a corresponding point of orientation in the second—to Fred's "How'd you meet that asshole Andy?" the fantasy supplies an elaborate description of the "job"; to "read what, Renee?" comes the answer "a fucking drivers' manual!" and so on—there remains in Pete's relationship with Alice something the fantasy cannot respond to and which, in its failure to do so, it provokes. At the moment we obtain what the prohibition had allowed us to imagine was lost, we instead encounter a Möbian void.

"You'll never have me". Alice delivers this devastating blow—strictly correlated with the abortive sex scene in the first part of the film—whereupon Pete transforms back into Fred, but it is a Fred who is apparently still in the thrall of the phallic exception. Amid the chaotic last fifteen minutes of the film, he finds Mr Eddy, bundles him into the car and drives him out into the desert. A question arises: why does he bring Mr Eddy to the exact same spot where Alice jilted him? We could read this bizarre undertaking as a kind of futile attempt to revive his wilting desire by bringing it into line with the law, using Mr Eddy to give a phallic inscription to the lack, to instate the paternal law as a stabilising factor.

The problem with this fantasmatic logic is that the phallic exception we took to guarantee the law turns out to be constructed at the site of its *lack* of a guarantee, the lack of an external reference through which the signifying structure could be apprehended as an ordered totality, sealed from the effects of the real. If Mr Eddy cannot function as such a guarantor, does this mean we need to assume that there's a bigger, meaner Mr Eddy who has the monopoly on what we're missing out on? The Lacanian answer is unequivocally no: the "secret of the law" (McGowan, 2007, p. 173) is that it is without foundation. There is no Mr Eddy of Mr Eddy, to paraphrase Lacan's key claim that there is no Other of the Other. In this connection, it should come as no surprise that Mr Eddy meets his demise in the hands of the Mystery Man, the bearer of this secret.

What the Mystery Man whispers in Fred's ear immediately after killing Mr Eddy is thus our familiar "one meaning less", the minus-one. Lacan was led to posit that although the symbolic order is lacking one signifier, there must necessarily be a signifier for that lack of a signifier, which he denotes with the matheme S(Ⱥ). To put it another way, what is whispered is Fred's *namelessness*. It is the signifier that announces the absence of a signifier that would finalise the subject's representation in language, the gap in the place of the signifier for which all other signifiers represent the subject, condemning the latter to an indeterminate value in the signifying network. An inaudible whisper is well suited to convey this necessarily "unpronounceable" signifier (Lacan, 2006, p. 694), designating the unimaginable point at which the signifying structure is exposed to the destabilising effects of the real.

Why there's no such thing as a bad coincidence

By means of a coda to this whirlwind tour of *Lost Highway*, it remains to be said that the incompleteness of the Other has far-reaching consequences. Starting out from this premise one can mark out a good deal of the Lacanian–Lynchian field. It is what throws us off-kilter as beings of language, and it does so in a way that makes itself felt at every level of what might loosely be called the structure's "scale", such that even the mildest disturbances in the unfolding of speech, or the flickering of a light, are marked by the point of abjection that one encounters in place of the final meaning one supposes to uncover at its zenith, leading Lacan to entertain the bizarre possibility that an utterance may only be of psychoanalytic value insofar as it trips up on itself or generates an incongruity (Lacan, 2006, p. 678).

Indeed, one such incongruity is provoked in the final scenes of the film, immediately after the "secret of the law" has been disclosed to Fred: investigating the crime scene at Andy's house, the detectives discover a photograph of Renee with Andy and Dick Laurent (as Mr Eddy is known to them, a small-time pornographer). While one could superficially argue that this is the moment the detectives solve the case—the discovery of Renee's involvement with Laurent sheds light on Fred's motive for killing her—this solution only holds insofar as it refers to an element that has been excluded: Alice, who was in the photo in a previous scene, does not appear in it when the detectives examine it. The only conclusion the detectives can muster comes in the form of Al's bizarre remark: "I think there's no such thing as a bad coincidence". The importance of this line is not to be found in the "I" of its statement (the "I" that thinks Renee's involvement with Laurent is no coincidence) but in its enunciation: the inclusion of the apparent redundancy "bad", which has no other function than to set the smooth elaboration of sense against the background of a fracture. If our detectives are to be cured of their passion for reality, it is a good place to cut the session.

References

Bristow, D. (2017). *2001: A Space Odyssey and Lacanian Psychoanalytic Theory*. London: Palgrave Macmillan.

Chion, M. (2006). *David Lynch*. London: Bloomsbury.

Dravers, P. (2004). "To Poe: Logically Speaking". In Ragland, E. and D. Milovanovic. *Lacan: Topologically Speaking* (pp. 205–224). New York, NY: Other Press.

Freud, S. (1915d). Repression. *S.E.*, 14. London: Hogarth.

Freud, S. (1912–1913). *Totem and Taboo*. *S.E.*, 13. London: Hogarth.

Freud, S. (1920g). *Beyond the Pleasure Principle*. *S.E.*, 18. London: Hogarth.

Greenshields, W. (2017). *Writing the Structures of the Subject: Lacan and Topology*. Palgrave Macmillan.

Henry, M. (1997). Le Ruban de Moebius: Entretien avec David Lynch. *Positif* 431: 8–13.

Herzogenrath, B. (1999). "On the *Lost Highway*: Lynch and Lacan, Cinema and Cultural Pathology". *Other Voices* 1: 3.

Lafont, J. (1986). *La topologie ordinaire de Jacques Lacan.* Paris: Points Hors Ligne.

Lacan, J. (1961–1962). *The Seminar of Jacques Lacan, Book IX: Identification.* Unpublished.

Lacan, J. (1977). *The Four Fundamental Concepts of Psycho-Analysis.* London: Hogarth Press.

Lacan, J. (1999). *On Feminine Sexuality, the Limits of Love and Knowledge, 1972–1973 (Encore).* New York, NY: W. W. Norton.

Lacan, J. (2006). *Écrits: The First Complete Edition in English.* New York, NY: W. W. Norton.

Lacan, J. (2014). *Anxiety. The Seminar of Jacques Lacan, Book X: Anxiety.* Cambridge: Polity.

Lynch, D. & B. Gifford. (1997). *Lost Highway.* London: Faber & Faber.

Morel, G. (2019). *The Law of the Mother: An Essay on the Sexual Sinthome.* London: Routledge.

McGowan, T. (2007). *The Impossible David Lynch.* New York: Columbia UP.

Nasio, J-D. (2004). "Object *a* and the Cross-Cap". In Ragland, E. and D. Milovanovic. *Lacan: Topologically Speaking* (pp. 98–116). New York, NY: Other Press.

Santini, C. D. (2017). *Lacan, Nous et le Réel.* <https://www.youtube.com/watch?v=AHGbL0zdVb8>

Žižek, S. (2000). *The Art of the Ridiculous Sublime: On David Lynch's Lost Highway.* Seattle, WA: University of Washington Press.

Zupančič, A. (2017). *What is Sex?* Cambridge, MA: MIT Press.

CHAPTER 8

"It is an illusion": the artful life of David Lynch

Allister Mactaggart

The Silencio nightclub scene in David Lynch's *Mulholland Drive* (2001) stands out for me. It is an affectively significant and pivotal quilting point within that film, and, I would suggest, a productive synecdoche for thinking about Lynch's overall creative oeuvre. Betty Elms (Naomi Watts) is awoken in the middle of the night by her lover, Rita (Laura Harring), sleep talking, and Betty is ordered to go with Rita somewhere "right now". Driven in a taxi through the nocturnal, disorientating strangeness of the city, they arrive at a location seemingly on the outskirts. Deposited at this liminal space called "Silencio" at a time which intermixes waking, sleeping, and dreaming, the interior of the club presents a similarly unconventional and uncanny nightclub setting, where a bizarre, *sui generis* performance begins, seemingly for their sole benefit as they take up their seats on the first-floor balcony, although there are a few other audience members in attendance as well, similarly silently transfixed upon the proscenium stage in front of them. These other figures in the auditorium may well stand in for the actual cinema audience watching the film who, like ourselves, find themselves drawn into this strange, dreamlike scene.

On stage, the Magician (Richard Green) declares:

> *No hay banda!* There is no band. *Il n'est pas d'orchestre.* This is all a tape recording. *No hay banda*, and yet we hear a band. If we want to hear a clarinet, listen … It's all recorded. *No hay banda*! It is all a tape. *Il n'est pas d'orchestre.* It is an illusion. Listen!

As Betty, Rita, and the audience (both those in the theatre as well as those watching the film) realise that what we see and hear is an artfully contrived "trick", we are all simultaneously interwoven into an even more complex, dialectical relationship with the "nature" of cinematic spectatorship. "It is an illusion", but, nevertheless, this does not dissipate the hold that the subsequent performance by Rebekah Del Rio of a Spanish language version of Roy Orbison and Joe Melson's song "Crying (Llorando)" has on Betty, Rita, and the audience, even though we see the performer collapse mid-song and the tape continue to play as she lies prostrate on the stage floor. Indeed, the artifice or illusion created is somehow amplified by our simultaneous acknowledgement and disavowal of the complexities of the "tricks" of cinema.

"It is an illusion" therefore makes plain a fact about film: it is carefully constructed using methods of film language to create an appearance of a "real" diegetic world into which we are drawn in the act of spectatorship. Often, in mainstream Hollywood films, these illusions create a semblance of "realism". However, in *Mulholland Drive*, the incongruities between the different levels within the film make such a level of reading difficult, if not impossible, to maintain. So it is difficult to know from whose "reality" we see and hear; and where we, as spectators, are situated at different times in the complexities of the interweaving narrative presented to us.

So when the Magician says "It is an illusion", what does this statement refer to? Is it purely what we see and hear on the stage, such as the sounds of "*un trombone à coulisse*", "*un trombón con sordina*", a "muted trumpet", or Rebekah Del Rio's subsequent performance, or is it something more? Various philosophical approaches have been employed by academics seeking to come to terms with the complexities of Lynch's films. For instance, Ronie Parciack, reading *Mulholland Drive* and *Lost Highway* (1997) through ancient Hindu and Buddhist schools of thought, argues that Lynch's films require a shift in the spectator's perspective from the

The Magician in Club Silencio, in *Mulholland Drive* (2001), dir. Lynch, courtesy of BFI Film Stills, Posters and Designs

ontological to the epistemological register; from that of pure being to that of knowledge. As such, she argues against psychoanalytic and other "depth psychology" approaches, in favour of readings that might chime more easily with Lynch's adherence to Transcendental Meditation (TM), itself derived from ancient Hindu philosophy. Parciack argues that an upheaval is required in the Western spectator's approach to Lynch's films, to provide

> [t]he new encounter with the phenomenal as ontologically dilapidated, and with the subject as unfixed and fluid, [which] may serve as an aperture to an adventure where film viewing is a point of departure that dismantles the subject's boundaries, widens its knowledge, releasing it from the constricting boundaries of the phenomenal.
>
> (Parciack, 2011, p. 89)

In the same collection of philosophical essays on Lynch's work, Mark Walling (2011, p. 97) adopts a Zen Buddhist approach to *Lost Highway*, against philosophical dualism, to argue that "for the Zen Buddhist, illusion means that the concept is not permanent or eternal and cannot substitute as a representation of reality". Therefore, he suggests, Lynch's "truth" as presented in the film is, like Zen Buddhism, an acknowledgement that by approaching things differently, by not seeking out logical, rational understanding, a deeper truth may be found, and further that Lynch's films provide a rich platform for such ideas to be experienced by the audience.

From a different philosophical perspective, that of Nietzsche and subsequent existentialism, Jennifer McMahon (2011, p. 116) argues that: "David Lynch's *Mulholland Dr.* not only illustrates the tendency that humans have to lie to themselves, it shows that our illusions are simultaneously tenuous and of tremendous consequence".

Support for such approaches can be ascertained from the source itself. In David Lynch and Kristine McKenna's memoir *Room to Dream* (2018, p. 206), it is stated that "the overarching theme in everything he's done is the issue of the dualities we live with and our efforts to reconcile them".

From analysing these various readings, we can clearly acknowledge how the openness to interpretation of Lynch's films provides for an array of philosophical approaches and readings to be fruitfully employed in discussing these texts. As Major Briggs (Don Davis) quotes from Shakespeare's *Hamlet* (1.5.167–168) to the assembled law enforcement officers in episode sixteen of the second season of *Twin Peaks* (1990–1991), after Leland Palmer (Ray Wise) is arrested for the murder of Laura Palmer (Sheryl Lee), but who subsequently dies in the police cell: "There are more things in heaven and earth than are dreamt of in your philosophy". Sigmund Freud also paraphrases this same quotation in "Delusions and Dreams in Jensen's *Gradiva*" (1907a, p. 17) with reference to the creative writer as an imaginative ally alongside the psychoanalyst. Freud also alludes to it in his essay on "Leonardo Da Vinci and a Memory of His Childhood" (1910c, p. 137). So there appears to be an initial unspoken correspondence between Freud and Lynch here, albeit from different viewpoints.

Freud/Lynch and creativity

From a psychoanalytic perspective Freud (1942a, p. 306) points out how in drama the spectator's enjoyment is based on an illusion, and how drama originated out of sacrificial rites such as the goat and the scapegoat in the cult of the gods. In Freud's analysis this theological connection was openly present in ancient times and still persists, albeit more well-hidden or suppressed, in the contemporary cultural arena. Allied to this is the lingering perception of the author of a text as the originator and guarantor of meaning. In a detailed reading of Freud's aesthetics, Sarah Kofman (1988, p. 10) demonstrates how Freud set out to unmask this theological conception of the artist as the father/god of the work. Furthermore, as Freud demonstrated in "The Moses of Michelangelo" (1914), "every text is tissue which masks at the same time as it reveals" (Kofman, 1988, p. 9).

Lynch has said on many occasions that: "What I would be able to tell you about my intentions in my films is irrelevant. It's like digging up someone who died four hundred years ago and asking him to tell you about his book" (quoted in Chion, 2006, p. 114). In a similar vein, "What Michelangelo himself would have to say about them [his works] is of little importance, because true intentions are not conscious" (Kofman, 1988, p. 10). Another possible link thus makes its way into our discussion of Freud/Lynch, inviting us to peek behind the curtain.

The unified field: Lynch's art in all its guises

Many studies of Lynch's work focus on his films and television productions, which is perhaps understandable, bearing in mind the greater knowledge of these aspects of his creative output. However, this may provide a distorted or partial perspective upon themes, images, and formal aspects from across his entire body of work. As is well known, Lynch started to make films after he experienced an epiphany in his painting studio at the Pennsylvania Academy of the Fine Arts in Philadelphia late one night in 1967 when, as he explains: "I'm looking at the painting and *from* the painting came a wind ... And the green garden plants began to move ... And I'm looking at this and hearing this and I say, 'Oh, a moving painting'. And that was it" (quoted in Cozzolino, 2014, p. 13). The creative reverie or epiphany experienced by Lynch at that moment of the seemingly still yet "living" painted image becomes the starting point for experimental adventures in film and television, which have held audiences spellbound and perplexed over several decades.

In his catalogue essay for the exhibition *David Lynch: The Unified Field*, held at Lynch's alma mater (although he only stayed there less than one year) in 2014, the curator, Robert Cozzolino, remarks that:

> Although the opposite has been asserted, Lynch is an *artist* who happens to make films as part of his expression. His identity as an artist is key to his work. His films are dependent on, flow from, and are inseparable from his identity as a visual artist; they are a painter's films, concerned with issues that arise from his sensitivity to composition, texture, formal relationships, and how subjects are enhanced by their presentation in a particular style. Lynch's integrative vision is related to his spiritual life, in particular his practice of Transcendental Meditation, which enables him to tap into his creative life in unexpected ways.
>
> (Cozzolino, 2014, pp. 14–15)

This "painterly" approach, coupled with an intuitive creative practice in a variety of media, allied to an unswerving meditation practice, provides for highly distinctive works that, in some respects, relate to other American and European art and films, but, at the same time, offer—with some notable exceptions, such as *The Elephant Man* (1980) and *The Straight Story* (1999)—a more complicated narrative trajectory, seemingly at odds with the generic certainties usually provided in such fare.

Maintaining this painterly approach to all of his work has been central to Lynch's creative practice. He has practiced twice-daily meditation since being introduced to the practice by his sister, Martha, in 1973. TM can be regarded as part of the Spiritual Regeneration Movement in the United States (Lynch & McKenna, 2018, p. 105). TM, rather than psychoanalysis, has been Lynch's preferred path through his life, creatively as well as personally, although he did once visit a psychiatrist seeking to address destructive patterns in his behaviour, but left almost immediately after ascertaining that the process could potentially affect or damage his creativity (Lynch, 2006, p. 61). Maintaining open channels to his creativity is central to Lynch's approach to all his work, in whatever medium. Lynch's adherence to TM and the teachings of the Maharishi Mahesh Yogi thereby brings together an artistic sensibility with a spiritual practice that developed in the United

States in the late eighteenth and early nineteenth centuries with Hindu classics such as *The Bhagavad Gita*, the *Upanishads*, and other Vedic texts being introduced via theosophists and transcendentalists like Ralph Waldo Emerson and Henry David Thoreau as a countercultural response to Christian evangelicalism. In the 1960s, *The Bhagavad Gita* (c. 1st–2nd century CE) again became an important part of "the efflorescence of another counterculture" (Fosse, 2007, p. xii), one in which Lynch's artistic and spiritual practices found a home.

Lynch's work has, however, attracted a great deal of attention from psychoanalytically-inspired writers, as it offers a great deal of food for thought about the complexities of the human psyche. Furthermore, Freud's writings are replete with references to art. As Kofman (1988, p. 38) points out, for Freud, "the model chosen to render dreams comprehensible is always art". When Freud took on the topic of "the uncanny" (1919h), he professed a reluctance to enter into the "negative" aspects of aesthetics in the face of professional aestheticians who were more "properly" interested in the elevated qualities of beauty rather than the disturbing verso of the topic which Freud investigated. The interests of the artist and psychoanalyst may appear to differ but as Kofman (1988, p. 191) also points out, "Though the psychoanalyst and the novelist arrive at the same results, they proceed differently".

For Lynch, as a young boy, drawing was something he thought you could do as a child but then would have to give up in adulthood. It was through meeting his friend Toby Keeler's artist father, Bushnell, in 1963 that he came to realise that being an artist was a realistic adult occupation. As part of his early artistic training Bushnell introduced Lynch to Robert Henri's book *The Art Spirit* (1984 [1923]), which became his "Bible" for living the "art life" (Rodley, 2005, p. 9). As Lynch and McKenna write (2018, p. 38), "The language and syntax of the book seem dated today, but the sentiment it expresses is timeless". Henri (1865–1929) was an influential painter and teacher whose own practice started in academic painting and impressionism before turning to "urban realist subjects executed in a bold, painterly style" (National Gallery of Art, Torchia, 2016). One can imagine the impact of Henri's words upon the young Lynch in that Henri had dedicated himself to "a life of uncontaminated devotion to art" (Watson, 1984, p. 5). Henri (1984 [1923], p. 15) declared that "Art when really understood is the province of every human being", as well as another quotation which one could imagine appealed to the nascent visual artist who struggled with verbal and written language: "Art after all is but an extension of language to the expression of sensations too subtle for words" (Henri, 1984 [1923], p. 87). So for Henri, as for Lynch, the art spirit provided the conditions for living the art life in which "the object is not to *make art*, but to be in the wonderful state which makes art inevitable" (Henri, 1984 [1923], p. 226). Additionally, for Lynch (2006, p. 2), TM provides the conditions in which he can "dive deeper in search of the big fish". These big fish being ideas—"The idea just needs to be enough to get you started, because, for me, whatever follows is a process of action and reaction" (Lynch, 2006, p. 12). This approach applies to all aspects of his creative practice, from films and TV to fine art and photography, design and music.

Art and sublimation

One does wonder though what Freud would have made of Lynch's recollections of discovering masturbation: "It was like discovering fire. It was just like meditation. You learn this technique and, lo and behold, things start changing and there it is. It's real" (Lynch & McKenna, 2018, p. 25). However, we can only surmise or fantasise how a session or two between Freud and Lynch might have turned out, if Lynch would stay that long! This seems to be an appropriate juncture to turn to Freud's concept of sublimation, the process by which the sexual instincts are diverted towards socially valued activities such as artistic creation. In his essay on Leonardo Da Vinci, Freud (1910c, p. 78) refers to how the sexual instinct has "the power to replace its immediate aim by other means which may be valued more highly and which are not sexual". Jacques Lacan extends Freud's rather underdeveloped concept further by linking creativity and art with the death drive, and provides a general formula for sublimation in that: "it raises the object [...] to the dignity of the Thing" (Lacan, 1992, p. 112).

The Lacanian psychoanalyst Darian Leader takes up Lacan's development of the concept in his book *Stealing the Mona Lisa: What Art Stops Us from Seeing* (2002) and points out that, for Lacan, sublimation refers "less [to] the myth of a sexual instinct than this idea of a zone of emptiness, of a void that is constitutive of our becoming human [...]

a zone that is always beyond what we can represent, or symbolize, or give meaning to" (Leader, 2002, pp. 58–59). So art is not always about trying to capture the beautiful, but it can be a veil or even verso, and can depict the ugly, the disgusting or disconcerting, the abject and the uncanny. Indeed, Lacan argues that in certain cases, as Leader (2002, p. 41) puts it, "What he [the artist] paints is there to attract the other, but to attract the other *away from him*". Furthermore, in this respect Leader also quotes Francis Bacon, one of Lynch's key artistic influences, who referred to painting as setting a trap; which Leader refers to as "a trap for the eye" and that art "is less the relaxed pastime of the aesthete than a furious defensive manoeuvre to ward off a malevolent Other" (Leader, 2002, p. 43).

In this regard "Lynch's own fearful, murky canvases", as Rodley (2005, p. xiii) describes them, would appear to demonstrate this desire to keep the malevolent Other at bay. The exhibition, *David Lynch: My Head is Disconnected*, shown at Home in Manchester (6 July 2019–29 September 2019) provided British audiences with an opportunity to see Lynch's artwork firsthand. Presenting an array of dark, disturbing images, seemingly full of fear and anger, and consisting of dark impasto paint, etchings, and mixed media, these works provide a useful insight into the range of Lynch's motifs and practices. One pertinent example is *Philadelphia* (2017), a large mixed media piece, which includes a photograph of the house he used to live in whilst residing in a run-down part of the city in the 1960s. Simultaneously frightening and "thrilling", Philadelphia provided a creative crucible for the young artist to encounter "darkness and confusion" and the resultant outlet that art can offer. As Lynch says in the documentary *The Art Life* (Barnes, Neergaard-Holm, & Nguyen, 2016): "I think every time you do something, like a painting or whatever, you go with ideas and sometimes the past can conjure these ideas and colour them, even if they are new ideas, the past colours them". Similarly, Freud points out that:

> A strong experience in the present awakens in the creative writer a memory of an earlier experience (usually belonging to his childhood) from which there now proceeds a wish which finds its fulfilment in the creative work. The work itself exhibits the elements of the recent provoking as well as the old memory.
>
> (Freud, 1908e, p. 149)

David Lynch and authorial trickery

However, Lynch's grappling with ideas/issues in his work, in a process of action/reaction, has been seen by critics and some audience members as a form of deliberate trickery by the author. This was particularly apparent when *Twin Peaks* was first shown on television. Adopting but challenging televisual conventions, the show led to accusations that Lynch (in particular, rather than Mark Frost) was playing with the audience, being deliberately obtuse and incomprehensible. So when we come to Lynch's films and work on TV, the perceived unintelligibility is seen by some as a form of cunning deliberately employed by him to confound or confuse his audience. For instance, the media theorist Henry Jenkins analysed how fans responded to *Twin Peaks* when it was first broadcast in 1990–1991, with the programme being one of the first where fans made extensive use of the then embryonic technology of internet discussion forums. Jenkins (1995, p. 66) remarks that: "Paradoxically, the more authority fans ascribed to the author, the more suspicious they became of that authority".

I've subtitled this chapter "the artful life of David Lynch" as an adaptation or play upon Lynch's references to the "Art Life". As an adjective, artful can mean "cunning; skillful, masterly; produced by art; dextrous, clever (archaic)" (Chambers, 1998, p. 86). Seen by many as deliberately cunning, Lynch's refusal to provide simple meanings for his work actually accords great respect for his audience, asking them to "feel" or "experience" it, which opens it up rather than closing it down, as so many generic films and television programmes do. Another example of Lynch's perceived trickery or artfulness is "David Lynch's 10 clues to unlocking this thriller [*Mulholland Drive*]". Provided with the DVD, it both intrigued and frustrated fans. Yet whilst there are some "truths" provided there in this teaser, the whole truth, if there is one, is to be more fruitfully sought out in the folds of the film itself.

Twin Peaks and the Anthropocene

This conjunction or (dis)connection between Lynch's perceived trickery or artfulness and childhood experiences/memories appears to present itself most forcibly in "Part 8: Gotta Light" of *Twin Peaks: The Return*

(2017), where Lynch and Mark Frost provide an origin myth for BOB, the manifestation of evil in *Twin Peaks*. In episode sixteen (directed by Tim Hunter) of the second season of *Twin Peaks*, Laura Palmer's murderer is revealed to be her father Leland Palmer, but inhabited by BOB (Frank Silva). For some this was seen as a cop-out, shifting the blame for this incestuous crime to an external source of "evil". After Leland's death in the prison cell, Special Agent Dale Cooper (Kyle MacLachlan), Sheriff Harry S. Truman (Michael Ontkean), and Albert Rosenfeld (Miguel Ferrer) go out into the woods, where they find Major Garland Briggs and discuss what they've witnessed, trying to make sense of the strange events that have taken place. After Briggs recites the lines from Shakespeare's *Hamlet* discussed earlier, Albert says "Maybe that's what BOB is, the evil that men do". Sheriff Truman then asks where BOB is now (as he has escaped) and subjective point of view shots show the spirit of BOB returning to the ancient woods surrounding the town of Twin Peaks as a figure of an owl flies towards the camera, bringing the episode to a close.

"Part 8: Gotta Light?" of *Twin Peaks: The Return* stands out (for me) as an outstanding, bravura piece of filmmaking in response to the question of where BOB is and how he came into being. This episode has the look and feel of a standalone experimental piece of art film, thereby linking Lynch's own artistic origins (creating a "moving painting") with an extraordinary recondite narrative solution as to how BOB's evil got into the world and came to infect small-town America. As usual with Lynch's work, this episode polarised opinion. However, I would suggest that Lynch and Frost's explanation for BOB is extremely pertinent, prescient, and "right on the money".

In a 2017 article about this episode, Walter Metz refers to its aesthetic links to the 1960s world of Stanley Kubrick and Stan Brakhage, whilst arguing that, at the same time, "it leads us narratively and thematically with great precision toward an explanation for the backstory of *Twin Peaks*". The formal, aesthetic, narrative, and thematic elements that Metz refers to are on to something, but I believe that this something is even more important than alluded to in this article.

The episode opens with Cooper's doppelgänger, Mr C (Kyle MacLachlan), on his journey in the middle of the night after escaping from jail. Subsequently shot by his accomplice, Ray Monroe

(George Griffith), mysterious "ghouls" emerge from the darkness to provide an extreme form of bloody heart manipulation that brings him back to life, and from his chest emerges the face of BOB. This terrifies Ray, who then drives away, leaving Mr C by the side of the road. However, following Mr C's resurrection, we switch to another location, and on-screen text tells us that it is "July 16, 1945, White Sands, New Mexico, 05:29 AM (MWT)". We then see the atomic test explosion that took place at that time as part of the Manhattan Project in the United States of America but supported by the British and Canadian governments, as the camera takes us from afar into the quantum midst of the subsequent aftermath for an extended experimental piece of filmmaking. In one of these bubbles of destructive energy we see the face of BOB appearing as an effect of the explosion. This highly abstract explanation for BOB's origins connects his evil directly to the first nuclear bomb test at Alamogordo, New Mexico, which was the first "successful" nuclear bomb test, code-named "Trinity". The main scientist behind the test, J. Robert Oppenheimer (1904–1967), apparently named it "Trinity" because of the English metaphysical poet and clergyman John Donne's (1572–1631) poem "Holy Sonnet XIV: Batter My Heart, Three-Personed God" (1633). When he witnessed the actual explosion Oppenheimer was also reminded of the Hindu sacred text, *The Bhagavad Gita*, at the point where the god "Lord" Krishna states to his interlocutor, Arjuna: "I am time run on, destroyer of the universe, risen here to annihilate worlds" (*The Bhagavad Gita*, 1994, p. 51).

During the footage of the explosion, Lynch uses accompanying music from Krzysztof Penderecki's "Threnody to the victims of Hiroshima" (1960), thereby linking this test to the subsequent horrors of the use of atomic bombs on Hiroshima and Nagasaki, less than a month after the Trinity test. Furthermore, as Metz (2017) points out, this use of music reinforces links with Stanley Kubrick's *Dr. Strangelove or: How I Learned to Stop Worrying and Love the Bomb* (1964). But it is this "successful" testing of the bomb on American soil to which Lynch and Frost attach BOB's arrival into the world. (And in a sense, any bomb test on native soil can be considered as a form of limited civil war, in that the immediate population is always affected, often censored and subject to illness, early deaths, and subsequent genetic disorders.)

For a number of geologists and thinkers, the Trinity test "marks the start of a new unit of geological time, the Anthropocene epoch" (Monastersky, 2015). The term derives from the Greek word *Anthropos* (human) and is used to refer to the dominant influence of human activity upon the environment. What is extraordinary about the growing consensus among geologists and others is the speed of change upon the earth due to human activity, and the devastating impact this is having in terms of climate change.

Different starting points are put forward by geologists for the Anthropocene. One is an "early Anthropocene" level some thousands of years ago which coincided with the beginnings of agriculture; a second level is proposed with the start of the Industrial Revolution in 1800, and a third in what is referred to as the "Great Acceleration" of the mid-twentieth century. In this respect, it is argued that the last of these "has the most pronounced and globally synchronous signal [...][with] an appropriate boundary level here to be the time of the world's first nuclear bomb explosion, on July 16 1945 at Alamogordo, New Mexico" (Zalasiewicz et al., 2015, p. 196). The authors suggest that "placing the benchmark at the first nuclear test provides a clear, objective moment in time" (Zalasiewicz et al., 2015, p. 200). Additionally, they point out that more than 500 nuclear tests were carried out since 1945 until a Test Ban Treaty came into effect in 1963, the result of these being that "This testing is the major cause of human-made radionuclides over the globe" (Zalasiewicz et al., 2015, p. 201).

Furthermore, the results of research presented at the 2019 General Assembly of the European Geosciences Union (EGU) provides evidence of "a ticking time bomb of buried nuclear material", which is being released by glaciers collapsing and melting into the ocean (Nield, 2019). The Lacanian analyst Janet Haney (2019, p. 215) remarks that: "We should not be surprised to hear that the discourse of capitalism has bitten a chunk out of the ice in the artic, like a mechanical jaw with an insatiable appetite". Haney goes on to argue that "against the machinery of the capitalist discourse we are going to need poetry" (2019, p. 215) and, I would argue, that "Gotta Light?" provides such a poetic response to the climate emergency that we are in the midst of. Indeed, it is such responses that can help to overcome the intractability of seemingly political impasses and Jacques-Alain Miller's phrase "there is a great disorder in the real" (quoted in Haney, 2019, p. 215). The Lacanian real being the order outside of symbolisation, linked together with the imaginary and the symbolic registers. *Twin Peaks: The Return* provides a poetic way of thinking about the impact and implication of human activity upon the planet, and is even more pertinent in its current iteration than it was in the show's first two seasons.

If we fast-forward towards the end of "Gotta Light?", we are shown another on-screen caption, this time eleven years further on from the Trinity test: "1956 August 5, New Mexico Desert". We see a young boy (Xolo Maridueña) and girl (Tikaeni Faircrest), seemingly in their early teens. The boy walks the girl home, in an innocent and coy display of adolescent sexual awakening. Interspersed with these shots are those showing the Woodsman (Robert Broski) going into the KPJK Radio Station. After the Woodsman's murder of the receptionist (Tracy Phillips) and the disc jockey (Cullen Douglas), and the broadcast of his mantra over the radio waves, which cause listeners to fall into sleep or a coma, we are then shown a large, strange, mutant insect, created as a result of the earlier test and the effect of the radionuclides now in the soil. The creature breaks out of its eggshell in the desert and makes its way into the room of the young girl we'd been introduced to earlier. The girl, who is sound asleep, ingests the insect through her open mouth, which presents eerie, disquieting images to the viewer. Special Agent Tamara Preston reports, in Mark Frost's paratext *Twin Peaks: The Final Dossier* (2017, p. 133), that the young girl is actually Laura Palmer's mother, Sarah Judith Novack, who moved to New Mexico in 1943, where her father worked as a Defence Department employee in some small but unspecified subcontractor role on the Manhattan Project. So the effect of the Trinity test in the New Mexico desert is shown to contaminate both the soil and the soul of the American nation just as surely it did when the bombs were subsequently dropped on Hiroshima and Nagasaki. A photograph of the Trinity test also adorns the wall of FBI Deputy Director Gordon Cole's (David Lynch) office, opposite a photograph of Franz Kafka, another key cultural influence upon Lynch. Richard Martin (2018) has also pointed out that a photograph of the Trinity test explosion is shown by the side of Henry Spencer's bed in *Eraserhead* (1977), thereby indicating the significance this event has had on Lynch's work over many years.

In a previous exploration of the role of landscapes in Lynch's work I had drawn attention to how these representations often chimed with others in the work of the transcendentalist and luminist painters of the nineteenth century, but that Lynch also shows us the underside of that surface beauty, such as the bugs under the carefully manicured and watered grass as in *Blue Velvet* (1986). I also suggested that the Log Lady (Catherine E. Coulson) from *Twin Peaks* "personifies the trauma inherent in the expansionist development of the country" as demonstrated by her log following the trauma of her husband's death. At that time, I concluded that "she offers an alternative to the patriarchal, capitalist destruction of nature and the landscape, if only we took time to listen to her message" (Mactaggart, 2013, p. 160).

Since then, however, knowledge of the rapidity of climate change has become much more apparent, and countries such as the United Kingdom, the United States of America, and others, have failed to stick to the Paris Climate Agreement reached in 2015. What's more, the United Nations Climate Change Conference (COP26) held in Glasgow from 31 October to 13 November 2021 has done little to offer us hope. As I write, the Brazilian president Jair Bolsonaro is permitting the laying waste of vast swathes of the Amazon rainforest in a more extreme version of neoliberalism that has been dubbed "uncontrolled predatory capitalism" (Albuquerque & Faria, 2019). Metaphorically, BOB in the guise of these political leaders is still running amok and causing untold damage to the planet. Activists such as Greta Thunberg and the school climate strikers, groups such as Extinction Rebellion, and other organisations have shown that urgent action is needed if we are to avoid imminent climate catastrophe. One might be tempted to argue that a television programme such as *Twin Peaks: The Return* will have a negligible impact upon the overall scenario, but I would suggest that Lynch and Frost's use of the Trinity test is a valuable (and perhaps unconscious) realisation that this act was of fundamental import to the world. Thus, the atomic bombing of Japan and the death of a fictitious girl in the Pacific Northwest of America are inextricably linked. As is the depiction of Laura Palmer's dead body wrapped in plastic, which is another signifier of the harm being done to the planet by the extensive misuse of this by-product of fossil fuel production (Leather, 2019); whilst, at the same time offering a "poetics of plastic", as I've discussed elsewhere (Mactaggart, 2010, pp. 31–33).

In the exhibition of Lynch's art at Home in Manchester in 2019, I was struck by *BOB's Anti-Gravity Factory* (2000, 120 × 105 cm). The painting depicts a three-storey factory made of cardboard with three belching chimneys floating above the ground, affixed to the surface of the painting above brown and muddy swirling, polluted land below, all set in an orange apocalyptic-looking background. In an article examining Maurice Blanchot's text of 1964, "The Apocalypse is Disappointing", and analysing "The Bomb" as a "genuine master signifier", Alenka Zupančič (2018, p. 24) argues "that we are not facing an approaching apocalypse, but rather already standing *within* it". *BOB's Anti-Gravity Factory* and *Twin Peaks: The Return* appear to echo these sentiments. Zupančič concludes, however, that what we need to do is to rediscover lost causes to be able to find a way forward. This calls for the "courage of the hopeless" (Zupančič, 2018, p. 29), and Lynch's creative output provides, I believe, a means for him to offer this to us.

David Lynch, *Bob's Anti-Gravity Factory*, 2000, oil and mixed media on canvas, courtesy of David Lynch

Lynch's art, in all its guises, provides a vehicle for him to explore ideas, stories, feelings, and moods in a highly creative and personal manner, but one which makes these visions available for us all to reflect upon what we see and hear. As Robert Henri (1984 [1923], p. 87) put it: "Art after all is but the extension of language to the expression of sensations too subtle for words". Freud's admiration for artists and the insights their work offers is clear throughout his exploration and development of the theory and practice of psychoanalysis. Art may indeed be an illusion, but it is one that can offer us, as in the use of the Trinity nuclear test in *Twin Peaks: The Return*, an invaluable insight into truths that may hitherto have been veiled or hidden.

Lynch's abstractions can thereby offer another route to the royal road of the unconscious. As Freud (1928b, p. 441) also remarked, "Before the problem of the creative artist analysis must, alas, lay down its arms". Furthermore, as Sarah Kofman (1988, p. 198) points out, Freud follows Aristotle in regarding an illusion as distinct from a falsehood: "By means of illusion, the artist—himself under an illusion—nonetheless tells the truth". As such, I would argue that Lynch's work, in all its guises, has always been truthful, and agree with Freud (1914b, p. 236) that "the artist is no less responsible than his interpreters for the obscurity which surrounds his work". So rather than regarding Lynch as artful, in the sense of being a deliberate trickster in his interactions with his audience, we can perhaps rephrase this relationship as an acknowledgement of the importance of a life lived full of art, and we can rejoice that Lynch, as Special Agent Dale Cooper might put it, is an artist; a fine artist; a damn fine artist.

References

Albuquerque, E. & Faria, C. F. (2019). Uncontrolled Predatory Capitalism: The Core of Bolsonaro's Government. *International Socialism* 164: 25–47.

Barnes, R., Neergaard-Holm, O., & Nguyen, J. (2016). *David Lynch: The Art Life* [DVD]. Absurda, Duck Diver Films, Hideout Films, and Kong Gulerod Film.

Bhagavad Gita (The) (1994), trans. W. J. Johnson. Oxford: Oxford University Press.

Chambers. (1998). *The Chambers Dictionary*. Edinburgh: Chambers Harrap.

Chion, M. (2006). *David Lynch*, (2nd edn), trans. R. Julian. London: BFI.

Cozzolino, R. (2014). *David Lynch: The Unified Field*. Philadelphia, PA: Pennsylvania Academy of the Fine Arts.

Fosse, L. M. (2007). Introduction. In *The Bhagavad Gita* (pp. ix–xxiv), trans. L. M. Fosse. Woodstock, NY: YogaVidya.com. <http://library.umad.mo/ebooks/b17771201.pdf> (last accessed 10 June 2020).

Freud, S. (1907a). Delusions and Dreams in Jensen's *Gradiva*. *S.E.*, 9: 7–40. London: Hogarth.

Freud, S. (1908e). Creative Writers and Day-Dreaming. *S.E.*, 9: 141–152. London: Hogarth.

Freud, S. (1910c). *Leonardo Da Vinci and a Memory of His Childhood*. *S.E.*, 11: 63–137. London: Hogarth.

Freud, S. (1914b). The Moses of Michelangelo. *S.E.*, 13: 211–235. London: Hogarth.

Freud, S. (1919h). The "Uncanny". *S.E.*, 17: 219–256. London: Hogarth.

Freud, S. (1928b). Dostoevsky and Parricide. *S.E.*, 21: 175–197. London: Hogarth.

Freud, S. (1942a). Psychopathic Characters on the Stage. *S.E.*, 7: 305–310. London: Hogarth.

Frost, M. (2017). *Twin Peaks: The Final Dossier*. London: Macmillan.

Haney, J. (2019). The Disorder of the Day: Climate Change and the Capitalist Discourse. *Get Real. The Lacanian Review* 7: 213–216.

Henri, R. (1984 [1923]). *The Art Spirit*. Boulder, CO: Westview Press.

Jenkins, H. (1995). "Do You Enjoy Making the Rest of Us Feel Stupid?": alt.tv.twinpeaks, the Trickster Author, and Viewer Mastery. In D. Lavery (Ed.), *Full of Secrets: Critical Approaches to Twin Peaks* (pp. 51–69). Detroit, MI: Wayne State University Press.

Kofman, S. (1988). *The Childhood of Art: An Interpretation of Freud's Aesthetics*, trans. W. Woodhull. New York, NY: Columbia University Press.

Lacan, J. (1992). *The Seminar. Book VII. The Ethics of Psychoanalysis, 1959–1960*. London: Routledge.

Leader, D. (2002). *Stealing the Mona Lisa. What Art Stops Us From Seeing*. London: Faber & Faber.

Leather, A. (2019). Why Capitalism Loves Plastic. In M. Empson (Ed.) *System Change Not Climate Change: A Revolutionary Response to Environmental Crisis* (pp. 140–148). London: Bookmarks.

Lynch, D. (2006). *Catching the Big Fish: Meditation, Consciousness, and Creativity*. New York, NY: Jeremy P. Tarcher/Penguin.

Lynch, D. & McKenna, K. (2018). *Room to Dream*. Edinburgh: Canongate.

McMahon, J. (2011). City of Dreams: Bad Faith in *Mulholland Dr.* In W. J. Devlin and S. Biderman (Eds.), *The Philosophy of David Lynch* (pp. 113–126). Kentucky, KY: University of Kentucky Press.

Mactaggart, A. (2010). *The Film Paintings of David Lynch: Challenging Film Theory.* Bristol: Intellect.

Mactaggart, A. (2013). Lynchian Landscapes and the Legacy of the American Sublime. In G. Harper & J. Rayner (Eds.), *Film Landscapes: Cinema, Environment and Visual Culture* (pp. 146–162). Newcastle-Upon-Tyne: Cambridge Scholars Publishing.

Martin, R. (2018). David Lynch sprawls. *Freud/Lynch: Behind the Curtain* Conference, 26–27 May. The Freud Museum in conjunction with the Rio Cinema, London.

Metz, W. (2017). The Atomic Gambit of *Twin Peaks: The Return. Film Criticism* 41(3). <http://dx.doi.org/10.3998/fc.13761232.0041.324> (last accessed 29 May 2020).

Monastersky, R. (2015). First Atomic Blast Proposed as Start of Anthropocene. *Nature News* (16 January 2015). <http://www.nature.com/news/first-atomic-blast-proposed-as-start-of-anthropocene-1.16739> (last accessed 29 May 2020).

Nield, D. (2019). A Huge Amount of Nuclear Fallout Is Embedded in Glaciers, and They're Starting to Melt. *Science Alert* (12 April). <https://www.sciencealert.com/there-s-a-bunch-of-nuclear-fallout-embedded-in-glaciers-and-they-re-starting-to-melt> (last accessed 29 May 2020).

Parciack, R. (2011). The World as Illusion: Rediscovering *Mulholland Dr.* and *Lost Highway* through Indian Philosophy. In W. J. Devlin and S. Biderman (Eds.), *The Philosophy of David Lynch* (pp. 77–91). Kentucky, KY: University of Kentucky Press.

Rodley, C. (2005). *Lynch on Lynch (Revised Edition).* London: Faber and Faber.

Torchia, R. (2016). Robert Henri. *National Gallery of Art.* <https://www.nga.gov/collection/artist-info.1391.html> (last accessed 29 May 2020).

Walling, M. (2011). All Roads Lead to the Self: Zen Buddhism and David Lynch's *Lost Highway.* In W. J. Devlin and S. Biderman (Eds.), *The Philosophy of David Lynch* (pp. 95–112). Kentucky, KY: University of Kentucky Press.

Watson, F. (1984). Introduction. In R. Henri (1984 [1923]). *The Art Spirit* (pp. 5–10). Boulder, CO: Westview Press.

Zalasiewicz, J. et al. (2015). When Did the Anthropocene Begin? A mid-Twentieth Century Boundary Level Is Stratigraphically Optimal. *Quaternary International* 333: 196–203. <http://dx.doi.org/10.1016/j.quaint.2014.11.045> (last accessed 29 May 2020).

Zupančič, A. (2018). The Apocalypse Is (Still) Disappointing. *S: Journal of the Circle for Lacanian Ideology Critique* 11: 16–30.

CHAPTER 9

David Lynch sprawls*

Richard Martin

> My family, my friend, I have criss-crossed this great land of ours countless times. I hold the map of it here, in my heart, next to the joyful memories of the carefree days I spent as a young boy, here in your beautiful town of Twin Peaks. From Alexandria, Virginia, to Stockton, California, I think about Lewis, and his friend Clark, the first Caucasians to see this part of the world. Their footsteps have been the highways and byways of my days on the road. My shadow is always with me, sometimes ahead, sometimes behind, sometimes to the left, sometimes to the right, except on cloudy days, or at night.

Motorcyclist Wally Brando's monologue in episode four of *Twin Peaks: The Return* (2017), performed with care and sincerity alongside his adoring parents, fast became a favourite moment for many fans of the series, inspiring memes, artworks, and other online tributes. In the midst of a dark, slow-moving, and apparently random succession of events, the

* An earlier version of this chapter first appeared in *NANO: New American Notes Online*, Special Issue 15, Fall 2019. Reprinted with permission.

scene felt like light relief—a brief, blissful respite from complete confusion. Yet, as ever with David Lynch, we should take most seriously those moments that appear to be most frivolous. For Wally's cameo speaks to the defining features of *The Return*: its hugely increased scope, its desire to map a terrain far beyond a single small town, its ambition to take in an entire nation, to drive, fly, and wander from coast to coast, highways to byways, at its own, highly irregular pace. In short, *The Return* sprawls; it spreads out across time and space in a manner rarely seen in Lynch's previous work.

This chapter explores how *The Return* sprawls, and what sprawl might mean. I'm interested in the numerous spaces and places the series shows us, and the psychological states that particular locations evoke. In so doing, I want to relate something of the extraordinary experience of watching *The Return*—to consider how it encourages a viewer to think and feel in strange, unconventional ways. How might this epic extension to the *Twin Peaks* project relate to an American history, and an American geography, that Lynch has been plotting throughout his career?

The original *Twin Peaks* series (1990–1991) began with a map—a drawing of a small community in the woods created by Lynch as a blueprint for potential storylines (Rodley, 2005, pp. 158–159). In the first two series and in the film *Twin Peaks: Fire Walk With Me* (1992), the action is almost entirely confined to this town. Indeed, this has been a strength of Lynch's best work: the intense focus he places on a single, bubble-like location—think of Henry's tiny room in *Eraserhead* (1977), with its humming radiator and severe claustrophobia, or Lumberton in *Blue Velvet* (1986), where we join Jeffrey Beaumont in discovering hidden thrills beyond billboard perfection (Martin, 2014, pp. 35–36). Lynch excels at tightly constructed environments, in creating small, intricately detailed worlds. In a typically astute observation, David Foster Wallace once likened Lynch to "the type of bright child you sometimes see who's ingenious at structuring fantasies and gets totally immersed in them but will let other kids take part in them only if he retains complete imaginative control over the game and its rules" (Wallace, 1998, pp. 151–152).

In *The Return*, the game—and whatever rules govern it—now operate across a vastly expanded board. While we occasionally occupy familiar Pacific Northwest locales like the Double R Diner, the Roadhouse, and the Great Northern Hotel, we're more often transported far beyond

Twin Peaks to the neon lights of Las Vegas or FBI headquarters in Philadelphia, to a glass cube in New York City, and a black box in Buenos Aires. We spend time in Buckhorn, South Dakota—much to Albert's dislike—and inside the Pentagon in Arlington, Virginia. We travel to the Nevada desert, where the bodies are buried, and to White Sands, New Mexico, where the bomb was tested. There's brief trips to Montana and Utah, and to a sinister diner in Odessa, Texas. Even east London is evoked through the unforgettable character of Freddie Sykes, who seems like a descendent of the Victorian cockney crew last seen in Lynch's *The Elephant Man* (1980).

This is a grand journey to fill Wally Brando with pride. But it's also indicative of a world escaping and exceeding its usual boundaries, spilling out in unexpected directions at uneven speeds. *The Return* often feels messy and chaotic. So many US states, and so many states of viewing—sadness, frustration, terror, boredom, confusion, hilarity. As the critic Sarah Nicole Prickett noted, in the most perceptive of the many online episode-by-episode responses to the series, in *The Return* "worlds diverge and are weirdly, sparsely populated" (Prickett, 2017). If the original *Twin Peaks* was characterised by a strong sense of place, *The Return* often seems to emphasise placelessness.

Why might sprawl be a useful term to understand *The Return*? To sprawl, as defined by the *OED*, means to "be stretched out [...] in an ungainly or awkward manner". This feels like a very Lynchian posture. From his early short film *The Alphabet* (1968), which declared "Please remember, you are dealing with the human form", Lynch has always paid close attention to strange bodily contortions. Think of the impossibly swaying, dying figure that Jeffrey discovers at the end of *Blue Velvet*, or the mutated croaking flesh that Henry fathers in *Eraserhead*. As the novelist Tom McCarthy has argued "Deformity, for Lynch, is never thematic". Rather it is "*instrumental*", producing "a whole prosthetic order [...] an ontological condition" (McCarthy, 2017, p. 135). What's more, for Lynch, our bodies always have an intimate link with technology, a "persistent biologizing of media", as Justus Nieland puts it (Nieland, 2012, p. 113).

This is of particular significance for the world of *Twin Peaks*. For television sprawls, and sprawling is what we do while we watch it. Films are tight and compact, just as cinemas provide a focused, upright architecture for our viewing. Television, however, and especially television in an age of streaming and boxsets, is looser and open-ended. It induces guilty feelings of laziness, wasted time and low-grade consumption. It evokes slouching and bingeing on a couch in slumbering states of fragmented attention.

Sprawl also has a distinct and relevant architectural definition, summarised by the *OED* as: "The straggling expansion of an indeterminate urban or industrial environment into the adjoining countryside". This is territory beyond traditional spatial terms such as city and suburb. As urban historian Dolores Hayden explains in her *Field Guide to Sprawl* (2006), we need a new language to analyse big box stores, fast food outlets, strip malls, junkyards, billboards, remote prisons, and themed restaurants—all, we might note, the kind of "indeterminate" locations seen in *The Return*. These built forms also provoke an ungainly physical response: when we see sprawl, Hayden says, "we react with sagging shoulders and clenched jaws". "The visual culture of sprawl", she adds, "should be read as the material representation of a political economy organized around unsustainable growth" (Hayden, 2006, pp. 10–13).

Sprawl, then, has a bad reputation. No one has a good word to say about it. As Robert Bruegmann notes in *Sprawl: A Compact History* (2006), "most of what has been written about sprawl to date has been devoted to complaints" (Bruegmann, 2006, p. 3). Sprawl, to its critics, is undisciplined and inelegant. It occupies time and space with ugly, disorganised forms. It scatters and wastes resources in a careless fashion. It's bad for the environment, and for our lazy, stretched waistlines.

Before considering how we might examine *The Return* in this context, there are two further concepts that provide a productive framework for understanding Lynch's latest work. The first of these was famously outlined by the Dutch architect Rem Koolhaas in his own sprawling essay: "Junkspace". "Junkspace" describes the soulless spaces of purgatory that now dominate our environment: corporate lobbies and convention centres, shopping malls and parking lots. Such spaces represent "the fallout" of modernisation, Koolhaas suggests—sterile, generic, and "a new gospel of ugliness" (Koolhaas, 2002, pp. 175–190).

More recently, the artist and theorist Hito Steyerl has written about "junktime"—an experience of the world as "wrecked, discontinuous, distracted" (Steyerl, 2017, pp. 21–29). Junktime, she explains, is "exhausted, interrupted, dulled by ketamine, Lyrica, corporate imagery" (p. 24). In a passage that feels extraordinarily relevant to *The Return*, Steyerl claims:

> If you tend to be in the wrong place at the wrong time, and if you even manage to be in two wrong places at the same wrong time, it means you live within junktime. With junktime any causal link is scattered. The end is before the beginning and the beginning was taken down for copyright violations.
>
> (p. 24)

Watching *The Return* often involves a similar sense of fragmentation and disconnect, as we encounter characters who always seem to be in the wrong place at the wrong time. The series is defined by temporal confusion, interrupted storylines, maddening breaks with narrative cause and effect, and a severe dulling of conventional screen momentum. It climaxes with a digitally-amended ending that loops back to undermine the very origins of the entire project. Such discontinuity might have been heightened depending on the initial viewing conditions. Did you sign up for a special subscription, rip off a friend's account, or watch a grainy, illegal stream? Was your experience wrecked by buffering and low-grade sound? Maybe, you didn't notice. Or perhaps you waited for the DVD boxset and had to endure many fearful months in which absent-minded scrolling or stray clicks might lead to a crushing spoiler. It's certainly not clear how any viewing experience of *The Return* could match the demanding cinematic screening conditions Lynch has often promoted for his films.

Yet *The Return* also feels resistant to junktime. It demands our full attention, and close scrutiny of its detailed and disorientating world. The images may lack the digital sheen of other contemporary television series, but they throb with imagination. Still, if you pay attention throughout the eighteen episodes of *The Return* expecting to be repaid with resolution, then you'll be grumpy and disappointed by the conclusion.

So, a sprawling landscape, filled with junkspace and governed by junktime: does this describe the third series of *Twin Peaks*? Let's consider the locations we visit in *The Return*. A trailer park where residents sell blood plasma for rent; a federal prison which looks like an Ikea store; endless shacks and dives and dingy interiors; long, straight roads through flat plains; car dealerships and filthy garages; shiny corporate offices with glass walls, leather chairs, and pained expressions; "a fucking morgue" where you can't even smoke, as Diane discovers. It's America, but it could be anywhere. "When you get there, you'll already be there", as they say in the Red Room. The locations seem mundane, but also strangely significant, and all are shot in the harsh, stark clarity of digital, where the original two series were soaked in warm, inviting film.

One particular location stands out as a literal manifestation of urban sprawl: Rancho Rosa, the desolate suburban scheme where Dougie lives, which also lends its name to the production company behind the series. This Double R development lacks all the charm of its Twin Peaks counterpart. Rancho Rosa, we're told, is a six-to-eight-dollar cab ride from the Vegas strip, but there's no casino glamour here. Surrounded by a high brick wall, and framed by a grubby billboard showing smiley white faces, Rancho Rosa is a post-crash nightmare: rows of uniform nondescript houses, only distinguishable by the colour of their front doors, divided by wastelands and potholed roads. It's a place for insurance salesmen to meet prostitutes and hitmen to hang out, for drug addicts to fester and for homeless people to roam with shopping trolleys. "Someone manufactured you", we might say to these deadening homes where foreclosure looms heavy. Even a car bomb can't liven up its drained, exhausted atmosphere. There's nothing rosy here, nor any trace of a ranch. A palpable—if deeply flawed—notion of community bound the original *Twin Peaks*; in *The Return*, no such assumption exists.

Dougie, bless him, looks at his suburban life as if it's the strangest, funniest thing in the world, which perhaps it is. He lives in his own kind of junktime—a painful, ungainly zone of borrowed gestures and awkward movements. Beyond Rancho Rosa, he's forced into the junkspace of Lucky 7 Insurance, loitering in a privatised plaza after a day spent on the beige carpets of his plush, mind-numbing office. What would this environment look like if you'd come from another world? It wouldn't feel lucky, that's for sure.

An innocent visitor might also ask: what produced this sprawling landscape? Lynch gives us a typically oblique answer in *The Return*. Episode eight of the series begins on the highway system then switches to the event that generated it: the first dropping of the Atomic Bomb in 1945, the birth of a new world. As Lynch's camera moves slowly towards the billowing explosion, we're immersed in its unfurling chaos of noise, dust, and fire. It's a catastrophe that's both deadly and generative; a shocking, shattering interruption; the ultimate glitch in space and time.

In the United States, there were twin architectural responses to the nuclear age. There was a passion for domes, epitomised by Buckminster Fuller and Shoji Sadao's famous 1960 proposal to encase midtown Manhattan—a desire to contain and shelter citizens, huddled together for protection. At the same time, and propelled in legislative terms by the 1956 Interstate Highway Act, there was the development of an elaborate national highway system, which would separate and scatter people in suburban developments, while allowing weapons to move around at high speed. Gordon Cole has a large picture of a mushroom cloud in his FBI office, and Henry in *Eraserhead* has one pinned to his wall, too. As ever with Lynch, history is manipulated and reworked in unexpected ways. The bomb reordered minds and worlds, *The Return* suggests, and that reordering was messy and complex, its consequences spawning, sprawling, and uncontrollable. Lynch's account of American geography contains no straight stories.

If the scattered locations of *The Return* might be seen as spatial sprawl, then the series also sprawls across time, its eighteen hours creating a form of durational aesthetics. Those hours are defined by slowness, a constant feeling of decoys and delays, which are often infuriating, sometimes unbearable, frequently hilarious. Everything takes too long in *The Return*. Scenes are stretched way beyond conventional televisual length: a barman sweeps the Roadhouse floor forever, a French woman just can't leave Gordon's hotel room, Audrey and her husband have interminable conversations. We seem to wait an eternity for Dougie to reawaken as Agent Cooper. Twenty-five years in the making, *The Return* is determined to highlight the experience of time passing.

The sprawling form of *The Return* gives it a unique feeling of fullness, a straggling expansion into new indeterminate zones. There's endless "room to dream", to borrow the title of Lynch's recent memoir (2018). We have extended access to secondary or tertiary characters; we hear in full the carefully-curated Roadhouse playlist at the end of each episode; we can study at length Harry Dean Stanton's extraordinary face. Such temporal sprawl can feel discomforting, but it also allows us thinking space between the intense and often violent encounters that pepper the series. Moments of quiet tenderness, longing, and sadness emerge. A project shadowed by illness and death—of cherished friends and long-term collaborators—is generous with its mourning process.

In this respect, the series makes the case for sprawl as a productive mode of thinking, especially when encountering the intricacies of a director's long career. Sprawl might offer a sense of getting lost in a world or of living with chaos and fragmentation. As a late work in the Lynchian canon, *The Return* provides its creator and his dedicated audience with ample space and time to imagine unexpected connections with past works. What else might link Henry and Gordon Cole, beyond an interest in the bomb? Perhaps Freddie's epiphany that his true destiny lies not in London but in Washington State suggests that Twin Peaks *is* somehow linked with the Victorian world of *The Elephant Man*. By this point in Lynch's life, the potential for critical cross-referencing and dreamy speculation are rich. As such, we might think of sprawl as a form of free association, allowing both spectators and filmmakers to explore memories and make imaginative connections.

There's a broader sense in which sprawl might help us approach Lynch's varied output across six decades. Responses to his work often pivot on questions of control and authority. Is watching Lynch about letting go, losing your inhibitions, and immersing yourself in visual and aural experimentation? Alternatively, is watching Lynch about maintaining a sharp, focused critical eye, noting clues and symbols, drawing connections and nodding at the cultural references?

Sprawl seems to transcend this divide. With its spatial and temporal expanse, with a plot that invites theories but is impossible to summarise, *The Return* asks us to think in a different way. In many respects, *The Return* acts as a summary of Lynchian obsessions—combining chunks of his work from art school and *Eraserhead* to *Inland Empire* (2006) and his online experiments. While this is true, it shouldn't stop us from confronting what's radically new here, and the challenges it poses.

To finish, though, let's return to the opening of the series. Of course, with Lynch, and with the *Twin Peaks* project in particular, we're never far away from a shadow or a double or a doppelgänger. There's one clear antithesis of sprawl in *The Return*: the densely packed New York cityscape Lynch introduces in episode one with one of his hypnotic aerial shots. Inside a loft, high in an ominous tower, we see the now-familiar symbols of urban artistic creativity: remnants of industrial labour via a clanking lift, exposed brickwork, and peeling paint, now housing a highly choreographed group of cameras trained on a glass cube, supported by an elaborate server. It's the perfect location for contemporary performance, and we have a select audience waiting for something to happen, unsure what might occur. It's also the perfect spatial metaphor for everyone watching at home, suspended on their sofas in anticipation. We expect avant-garde experimentation to take place in a location like this—a gentrified warehouse space in a hip urban centre.

But once this cube has unleashed its grisly spirit, the loft is not a location where Lynch wants to linger. He barely bothers to return. Turn your attention to other highways and byways, the series suggests. Get out of New York and criss-cross this great land. It's a restless, sprawling spirit epitomised by the good wishes given to Wally Brando: "May the road rise up to meet your wheels".

References

Bruegmann, R. (2006). *Sprawl: A Compact History*. Chicago, IL: University of Chicago Press.

Hayden, D. (2006). *A Field Guide to Sprawl*. New York, NY: W. W. Norton & Co.

Koolhaas, R. (2002). Junkspace. *October* 100: 175–190.

Lynch, D. (2018). *Room to Dream*. Edinburgh: Canongate.

McCarthy, T. (2017). *Typewriters, Bombs, Jellyfish: Essays*. New York, NY: NYRB.

Martin, R. (2014). *The Architecture of David Lynch*. London: Bloomsbury.

Nieland, J. (2012). *David Lynch*. Chicago, IL: University of Illinois Press.

Prickett, S. N. (2017). Peak Peaks. *Artforum* 2 (September). <https://www.artforum.com/slant/sarah-nicole-prickett-on-twin-peaks-the-return-the-complete-recaps-70896>

Rodley, C. (2005). *Lynch on Lynch (Revised Edition)*. London: Faber & Faber.

Steyerl, H. (2017). *Duty Free Art*. London: Verso.

Wallace, D. F. (1998). *A Supposedly Fun Thing I'll Never Do Again: Essays and Arguments*. Boston, MA: Back Bay.

CHAPTER 10

Waiting for Agent Cooper: the ends of fantasy in *Twin Peaks: The Return*

Todd McGowan

Stuck in Deer Meadow

One of the clearest clues that Lynch provides about making sense of *Twin Peaks: The Return* (2017) is completely unremarkable and almost unnoticeable. In *Fire Walk With Me* (1992), Lynch locates the Fat Trout Trailer Park in the town of Deer Meadow, Washington, in the southwestern portion of the state. This is the town where Leland Palmer (Ray Wise) killed Teresa Banks (Pamela Gidley) after she attempted to blackmail him. In the third season of the series, the Fat Trout Trailer Park (now with the term "new" affixed haphazardly to its name), is in a different part of the state in Twin Peaks. The manager, Carl Rodd (Harry Dean Stanton), who worked at the trailer park when it was in Deer Meadow, has travelled with it. This relocation has caused some confusion among fans and even one creator of the show, as Mark Frost claims that it never moved at all in *The Secret History of Twin Peaks* (2016). But relocating the Fat Trout Trailer Park to Twin Peaks serves as a clue that Twin Peaks is not what it was before. It now resembles Deer Meadow much more than the Twin Peaks of the show's first two seasons.

In Deer Meadow, unlike in the Twin Peaks of the first two seasons, one constantly confronts the opacity of the Other. It is never clear how to understand the events that take place. No one is welcoming nor provides any answers to the questions that characters pose. No one offers hot coffee or cherry pie to visitors as they do in Twin Peaks. When FBI agents Chester Desmond (Chris Isaak) and Sam Stanley (Kiefer Sutherland) investigate the murder of Teresa Banks in Deer Meadow, they encounter nothing but obfuscation and silence, even from the local police. It appears as a town completely bereft of enjoyment, as suggested by the contrast between the sparse and unappealing Hap's Diner there and the welcoming Double R Diner in Twin Peaks. The Deer Meadow portion of *Fire Walk With Me* in the first thirty minutes of the film reflects a world in which one has no way of finding any enjoyment or even locating oneself.

In his films—this structure comes to a head in *Fire Walk With Me*—Lynch establishes a clear contrast between excessive worlds of fantasy teeming with enjoyment and sparse worlds where desire appears detached from any possibilities for realising itself (McGowan, 2007)—that is, between Twin Peaks and Deer Meadow. This opposition between plenitude and lack enables Lynch to create a distinction in the artistic world where none exists in ordinary experience. In everyday life, we rarely experience the excesses that populate Twin Peaks, nor do we endure the barrenness of Deer Meadow. We live in some amalgamation of the two most of the time. By separating these worlds, Lynch reveals the role that fantasy has in making this ordinary experience meaningful. Rather than serving as a retreat from a harsh reality, fantasy provides, in the world of *Twin Peaks*, the basis for our reality through the structures of satisfaction that it establishes. *Twin Peaks* (1990–1991) offers moments of transcendence that lift characters out of their everyday reality and that carry spectators with them, which is one reason why the series had such devoted followers. Lynch shows not only that fantasy has an essential function for us but also that its exploration offers a privileged avenue to understanding how subjects satisfy themselves.

The first two seasons of *Twin Peaks* and most of *Fire Walk With Me* highlight the productive power of fantasy: its ability to create events that would be impossible without it. Fantasy's basic function is to orient our desire, to give our desire a structure. Fantasy gives our desire a path to follow. As Jacques Lacan points out in his *Seminar VI*, "The function of fantasy is to provide the subject's desire with its proper level of correction or situation. This is why human desire is fixed, attached, and coapted, not to an object, but always essentially to fantasy" (2019). As it gives desire a path, fantasy simultaneously points to desire's possible realisation in an object that would create plenitude. Through the turn to fantasy, we are able to go beyond the limits that restrict our ordinary experience. In this way, fantasy delivers the impossible—or what is impossible within our present social reality. We can see characters transcend their usual situation in order to achieve a sublime connection with others that would be completely unthinkable outside the space of fantasy created in *Twin Peaks*.

For instance, in the first episode of the second season of *Twin Peaks*, Major Briggs (Don S. Davis) sits for coffee with his son Bobby at the Double R Diner. Up to this point in the series, the relationship between the two is almost non-existent. Major Briggs devotes most of his time to his military career and its discipline, while Bobby rebels by turning to drugs and criminality. Major Briggs appears to be a distant father, and Bobby seems to have no affection for him. Despite their familial relationship with each other, they have no bond at all. There is no emotional bond that links the moral sensibility of Major Briggs with Bobby's criminal recklessness. But in this scene, an intense connection emerges when Major Briggs tells Bobby the vision that he had the night before. When he begins to recount this vision, we see Bobby looking at his father sceptically. But as he continues, the reaction cuts to Bobby revealing how much this vision moves him. The vision starts with an account of a home where Major Briggs had once lived, but in the midst of it he describes his son knocking on the door. Then, he says to Bobby, "My son was standing there. He was happy and carefree, clearly living a life of deep harmony and joy. We embraced, a warm and loving embrace, nothing withheld. We were, in this moment, one". When Major Briggs reaches this conclusion, the cut to Bobby's face shows that he now feels this connection to his father as well, and yet nothing in the series foreshadows it.

This proclamation and the moment that it engenders are the products of the fantasy world that *Twin Peaks* creates. If *Twin Peaks* were a realistic television series, such a moment would appear camp. But in the fantasmatic world that the series presents, Lynch enables us to take such a moment seriously, and perhaps to cry with Bobby. When we are immersed in a fantasy world, we can transcend the limits that govern our everyday reality. Such moments are not a flight from reality but reflect fantasy's ability to take us beyond its limitations.

The psychic distance that separates a strict father from his wayward son in their social reality disappears when they enter the realm of fantasy. Such moments of fantasmatic connection pop up throughout the first two seasons of *Twin Peaks* but, importantly, have no place in *The Return*. While *Twin Peaks* in its initial incarnation illustrates the power of fantasy to enable a transcendence of limits, *The Return* makes clear that this transcendence itself has limits and that these limits derive from the structure of fantasy itself. Fantasy cannot ultimately save us from loss but creates the structure through which we can unconsciously repeat loss. The transcendence that it provides occurs only through a fundamental loss that it necessarily repeats. The problem with the first two seasons of *Twin Peaks* is that they arrest the logic of fantasy before this logic reaches its own internal impasse. We see plenitude without the loss that makes evident the necessity of loss and its repetition.

But the exploration of fantasy that occurs in *The Return* is confined to the season's final episodes. The situation of desire without a corresponding fantasy that begins *Fire Walk With Me* also confronts the spectator of *The Return*, except that rather than enduring only thirty minutes, it lasts almost the entire eighteen episodes.[1] Though the Double R has not become as bleak as Hap's Diner, it has spawned franchises and thus no longer serves as a site of singular satisfaction. The copies of the Double R signify the dilution of the *Twin Peaks* fantasy world. The dearth of fantasy space explains the small role that the titular town has in *The Return* as well. Twin Peaks has become a peripheral setting in relation to Las Vegas and New York. What's more, however, the third season figures Twin Peaks as a site of inexplicable obscurity, an obscurity that extends

[1] The prolonged submission to an experience of desire without any fantasmatic resolution on the horizon led a group of the show's fans to turn against *The Return* as evidence of Lynch turning toward complete self-indulgence. The *ne plus ultra* of this position is that of Jim Geraghty, whose essay on the series appeared in the *National Review* (2017). According to Geraghty, "*Twin Peaks* built its impassioned fan base on a traditional narrative, and the creators exploited the enthusiasm for that old style to ensure the creation of this new, very different, often deeply dissatisfying product".

beyond the confines of the town throughout the world depicted in the series. Major events occur in near-total opacity, while moments of clarity emerge only through absurdity.

When *The Return* does provide more information than the first two seasons do, it does so in a way that destroys the fantasy space of the first two seasons. This is what happens with Diane Evans (Laura Dern). Through the first two seasons, Diane exists only as an absence in the series. Agent Cooper (Kyle McLachlan) records memorandums that he sends to her, but she has only a fantasmatic existence for spectators. Nonetheless, her absence helps to produce a full world in the series. Cooper's way of addressing her suggests her understanding and competence, which in turn makes Cooper clearer as a character. She is an absence that fills out the fantasy world.

Diane's brief appearance in episode six identifies her but leaves her character mysterious. In the following episodes, she turns out to be nothing like what we would expect on the basis of hearing Agent Cooper talk to her in the first two seasons. Diane only grudgingly cooperates with Gordon Cole (David Lynch) and expresses open disdain for Tammy Preston (Chrysta Bell) when she meets her. In the final episodes, we discover that Diane is not really Diane at all but a tulpa, a duplicate created by Cooper's doppelgänger that assumes her identity. Diane's appearance in the third season thus marks a turn away from her role in the first two seasons but not in a way that gives her a fantasmatic status. Instead, she is another site that disappoints and misleads the spectator. The revelation of her identity, far from filling out an emptiness of the series, serves only to highlight how much we don't know about her.

By stripping away the fantasy elements from most of the running time of *The Return*, Lynch places spectators in a perpetual state of wonder, a state that prompts hours of collective speculation among fans of the show about the significance of what transpires.[2] Much more than the first two seasons of *Twin Peaks*, *The Return* marks a consistent refusal of clear sense, so much so that many adherents of the original series

---

[2] See, for instance, "Twin Peaks and David Lynch Forums", https://welcometotwinpeaks.com/discuss/.

soon gave up on trying to follow it.[3] Despite the mystery surrounding the death of Laura Palmer (Sheryl Lee) and the strangeness of the events that occur, the first two seasons have an abundance of sense. There is too much sense to be made, not too little, which contrasts the two moments of the series. Sense is precisely what fantasy provides. It gives the randomness of social reality an underlying narrative coherence that it otherwise lacks.[4]

The third season begins in the White Lodge with the Fireman (Carel Struycken), formerly known as the Giant, addressing FBI Agent Dale Cooper and telling him, "Listen to the sounds". After he says this, an indecipherable scratching sound repeats from the old gramophone on the table. The Fireman follows this up by stating, "It is in our house now ... It all cannot be said aloud now. Remember 430. Richard and Linda". Dale responds, "I understand", which certainly doesn't speak for the spectator, who is undoubtedly bewildered at this point. After the Fireman tells Dale that he is far away, Dale disappears, and the scene switches to the normal reality of Twin Peaks, where Dr Jacoby (Russ Tamblyn) receives a shipment of shovels.

Though we eventually learn the purpose of the shovels, the mystery of what the Fireman tells Dale endures throughout the season. There is no reason why "it all cannot be said aloud now" except that this mystery sets up the desire of the spectator by setting up a point of unknowing. The Fireman establishes a mystery for the sake of establishing a mystery, one that is resolved in the final episode, when Dale and Diane travel 430 miles, check into a hotel to have sex, and wake up the next morning seemingly transformed into Richard and Linda (at least according to the note that Diane leaves for Dale, which is addressed to Richard from Linda). At this point, the references from the Fireman's mysterious initial statement become clear, but the resolution is not at all a happy one. Realising the desire that begins the season doesn't lead to the salvation of Laura Palmer or the defeat of the supposedly negative force of Judy.

---

[3] One theoretically inclined friend of mine said to me, "I gave it a couple of episodes, but it soon became clear that there was nothing there". Many echoed versions of this same sentiment to me.

[4] This is why Slavoj Žižek claims that "fantasy is the primordial form of *narrative*". Slavoj Žižek, *The Plague of Fantasies* (London: Verso, 1997), 10.

Instead, it leaves Dale and the spectator stuck in a repetition that recreates the very force it attempts to destroy.

At this point, we see what the realisation of the fantasy played out in *The Return* looks like. The fantasy that structures this season is the salvation of Laura. This is a fantasy that becomes fully apparent only with Agent Cooper's awakening in episode sixteen and the events that follow. The final defeat of the forces responsible for loss—both BOB and Judy—does not eliminate loss. Rather than saving Laura and delivering them from loss altogether, the path to salvation that Cooper plots leads only to its repetition. In this way, *The Return*, by playing out the logic of fantasy to its end point, shows how fantasy exposes the inescapability of traumatic loss.

Throughout the series, Laura Palmer functions as the lost object within the collective fantasy. She has this role only insofar as she is lost, which is what *Fire Walk With Me* makes clear. When she is alive, she is just a normal troubled teenager. Her loss, however, enables her to function as the object within the fantasy that structures the world of *Twin Peaks*. She serves as the point of complete enjoyment that can never be recovered because it exists only through its loss. And yet the FBI inquiry into her death holds out the promise of providing recompense for the loss by identifying her murderer. Like all criminal investigations and punishments, it stems from the fantasy of recompense for loss.

Loss is the engine for desire and thus poses a constant problem for the subject because no object can eliminate it. Desire cannot realise itself through overcoming loss without destroying itself as desire. Fantasy, however, stages a solution to this problem of desire by tracing a path toward the realisation of desire via an impossible object that one could find while it remains lost. As Juan-David Nasio points out, "The function of the fantasy is to substitute for an impossible real satisfaction a possible fantasised satisfaction" (Nasio, 2005, p. 13). Fantasy imagines the realisation of desire because it translates the impossible lost object into an empirical object that has been lost. In the case of *Twin Peaks*, this is Laura Palmer. The world of *Twin Peaks* in the first two seasons is structured around Laura Palmer as the lost object. Without this fantasmatic support, desire has no path to its realisation. It has no way to gain its bearings.

Agent Cooper is the agent for the recovery of the object and the rectification of loss. In the second season, he solves the mystery of Laura's murder, but she nonetheless remains lost. *The Return* depicts his attempt to go beyond solving her crime and to recover the lost object completely, to save Laura from BOB and her early death. This is an impossible quest, and yet it is the end point of every fantasy. Only by following fantasy to this end point, as Lynch does in *The Return*, do we see how it necessarily leads to its inherent impasse. This impasse reveals the limits of Agent Cooper's power within the realm of fantasy. The salutary power of Agent Cooper disappears in *The Return*. While the first two seasons leave him overtaken by BOB at the conclusion, the ending of the third season reflects a much grimmer situation. His attempt to have the lost object by saving Laura from death at the hands of her father ends up repeating the trauma that she undergoes rather than saving her from it.

A dismal return

Twin Peaks: The Return leaves us stuck as spectators in the position of the desiring subject with only momentary glimpses of a resolution to that desire. Not only do bizarre and probably ultimately inexplicable events constantly take place, but even the central figure of the series, Dale Cooper, does not know who he is throughout most of the running time of the season. After the twenty-five years pass and Dale is set to return to his earthly existence and take the place of the evil doppelgänger Mr C (Kyle McLachlan) who had replaced him, Mr C refuses to return to the Lodge and cede his place to Cooper. As a result, Cooper cannot just enter directly back into existence. Instead, he replaces the replica (or tulpa) that had taken his place, Dougie Jones (Kyle McLachlan). But Cooper enters without any conscious knowledge of who he is or even how to interact with others in the world.

The greatest frustration among spectators of *The Return* surrounds the character of Dougie. He is unable to formulate his own words or act on his own but can only repeat words that he has heard. When he first emerges, he wins thirty large jackpots at the slot machines of the Silver Mustang Casino. But there is clearly no skill involved: he barely understands how to pull the lever and fails to try to collect his winnings as they pour from the machines. Things don't improve when he goes home to his family of Janey-E (Naomi Watts) and Sonny Jim (Pierce Gagnon). There is no gradual emergence of Cooper from Dougie, as one might expect. One watches him for episode after episode, waiting for the character of Dale Cooper to emerge, trapped in a constant disappointment.

There are moments that trigger Agent Cooper, however. When assassin Ike Stadler (Christophe Zajac-Denek) surprises him and tries to kill him, Cooper instinctively defends himself and subdues his attacker, assuring the spectator that Dougie has some relationship to Cooper. His wherewithal in the situation shocks Janey-E, who treats him like a helpless toddler most of the time. Lynch leaves Cooper in the helpless Dougie state for so long in order to enhance the spectator's desire for Cooper to emerge. The fantasy of FBI Agent Cooper as the figure of heroic salvation animates *The Return*, and the persistence of Dougie nurtures this fantasy.

While spectators wait for Agent Cooper's re-emergence from Dougie, they also follow Gordon Cole's attempt to locate and rescue Cooper. This quest leads Cole to Mr C and to Diane, but he only indirectly contributes to Cooper's awakening when the latter hears his name on the television. For spectators, both paths to Cooper seem like dead ends until this moment. This sharpens the contrast between *The Return* and the earlier seasons of the series.

The first two seasons of *Twin Peaks* (until the solution of Laura Palmer's murder) develop Laura as the ultimate fantasy object. Then *Fire Walk With Me* explodes this fantasy by showing the world from the perspective of the fantasy object herself (McGowan, 2007). But *Fire Walk With Me* leaves intact the figure of Agent Cooper in the fantasy, as the one who might save Laura, at least posthumously, from male sexual violence. Cooper's small role in *Fire Walk With Me* leaves his fantasmatic status intact.

But *The Return* does to the figure of Agent Cooper what *Fire Walk With Me* does to Laura: it reveals that his effort to rescue Laura—and the efforts of men like him—is actually part of the violence done to her, not a remedy for it. Rather than providing salvation, he exacerbates the problem. To put it in contemporary parlance, the "good guy with a gun" is the hidden support of the "bad guy with a gun" rather than a necessary counterweight. Though we wait for Dale Cooper to emerge for almost the entire season, the final two episodes reveal the nefariousness of this fantasy figure. When we get what we were fantasising about, things become worse rather than better.

This is because the elimination of BOB and phallic violence does not produce a perfectly satisfying world. Even if Cooper were able to defeat BOB once and for all, he would always have to contend with another source of evil. This is what Lynch shows through the depiction of Sarah Palmer (Grace Zabriskie) in *The Return*. In the first two seasons of the series, Sarah was always a victim herself or a bystander who unconsciously allowed Leland's rapes of Laura to continue without intervening. She was never a figure of malevolence herself. But this changes in *The Return*.

In episode fourteen, we see Sarah drinking alone at the Bang Bang Bar with a stereotypical "redneck" seated at a table a few feet from her. After a few moments, the dishevelled and dirty man with a t-shirt displaying "Truck You" approaches her and begins to flirt with her, saying "Are you drinking all alone tonight?" She responds, "Mind your own business, please". This prompts his outrage. After she asks him to sit down where he was, he begins to raise his voice and says "I'll sit wherever I want. It's a free country. It's a free *cunt*-ry". As he says this last insult, the camera captures him in a close-up, to emphasise the violence inherent in the expression itself.

He speculates that she is "one of those bulldykes", one of the "lesbos" who "like to eat cunt". After he says this, Sarah turns without any emotion and proclaims, "I'll eat you". He responds by saying, "I'll pull your lesbo titties off". Lynch cuts to a straight-on shot of Sarah, who reaches up, pulls her face off, and exposes a swirling, dark cauldron. She says in an altered voice, "Do you really want to fuck with this?" When she puts her face back on, she thrusts forward and takes a bite out of the trucker's throat. In the aftermath, she acts as if she has no idea what has happened, even though it was her act.

This moment foreshadows Dale's failure in the final episode. Even if he violates time and successfully saves Laura from phallic violence, he cannot rescue her from destructiveness itself. In this scene, Sarah herself overcomes this violence, but she does so by exercising an even more lethal violence. As she takes her face off, we see another force acting through her that subsequently eats the man's throat. She thwarts his display of male aggression but does not do so by eliminating violence. Her destructiveness is much more terrifying than his. Despite outmanoeuvring BOB, Cooper has no way of saving Laura from this form of violence.

But in order to show the ultimate deleterious effect of Agent Cooper, Lynch first builds up our desire for his emergence and then gives a full fantasmatic weight to his initial appearance as himself. Hospitalised after electrocuting himself when he hears the name "Gordon Cole" while *Sunset Boulevard* (1950) is on television in episode sixteen, all of a sudden Dougie comes out of his coma and reveals himself to be Dale Cooper. For one of the few times in *The Return*, we hear the "*Twin Peaks* Theme" used to indicate a fantasmatic moment of ecstatic enjoyment. While the first two seasons of the series often used the "*Twin Peaks* Theme" to indicate an enjoyment or a suffering that went beyond the bounds of everyday reality, Lynch rarely uses it in season three precisely because such moments are almost non-existent.

Dale's return from the figure of Dougie is the return that the title of the series alludes to. The spectator enjoys the long-awaited return of Agent Cooper as the fantasmatic resolution of the desire that the entire season has established. As Cooper walks out of the hospital room, Dougie's boss Bushnell Mullins (Don Murray) asks him, "What about the FBI?" Lynch cuts to a medium shot of Dale, who responds, "I am the FBI". As he says this, the "*Twin Peaks* Theme" begins to swell to create a sense that salvation has finally arrived. This is the first truly fantasmatic moment in a season that, in direct contrast to the first two, is bereft of such moments.

World without fantasy

Although *The Return* includes most of the characters from the first two seasons, Lynch no longer depicts them in the same way. Instead of creating a fantasy realm in which the impossible can happen, the appearance of the disparate characters of the *Twin Peaks* world serves only to reveal the incoherence of this world. There are no more opportunities for connections like the one that occurs between Major Briggs and Bobby. *The Return* depicts a world of isolated beings that lack the coordinates for connecting with each other. This radical change from the earlier seasons indicates that we have left the immersion in a fantasy space for a desert of isolated, desiring beings. Without fantasy, there are no moments of connection because there is no transcendence of the self.

This is clearest in the case of Wally Brando (Michael Cera), the son of Andy (Harry Goaz) and Lucy (Kimmy Robertson). Although Wally does not appear in the first two seasons, his return home in the third season repeats the same dynamic that we see between characters there, but with a totally different result. Given our experience with the series, we might expect Wally's return home to spark a moment of transcendence. In the first two seasons, improbable moments of unforeseen connection take place between characters, such as the diner scene between Major Briggs and Bobby. We see characters alienated from each other experience a sublime moment in which they overcome the constraints of their situation. For instance, this occurs between Twin Peaks Sheriff Harry S. Truman (Michael Ontkean) and FBI Agent Albert Rosenfield (Miguel Ferrer). Albert constantly provokes Harry with his dismissive rudeness toward the backwardness of Twin Peaks. This leads Harry to punch him on one occasion. As the hostility between them increases, Albert continues the insults. When Harry asks Agent Cooper what needs to be done, Albert cracks, "You might practice walking without dragging your knuckles on the floor". This prompts Harry to threaten Albert with an increase in violence.

Precisely at this moment of extreme antagonism, Albert walks towards Harry. A fight seems sure to ensue. We see their faces inches apart, looking at each other in a close-up. But rather than attack Harry, Albert launches into a completely unexpected proclamation of nonviolence and love. He says

> You listen to me. While I will admit to a certain cynicism, the fact is that I am a naysayer and hatchet man in the fight against violence. I pride myself in taking a punch, and I'll gladly take another because I choose to live my life in the company of Gandhi and King. My concerns are global. I reject absolutely: revenge, aggression, and retaliation. The foundation of such a method … is love. I love you, Sheriff Truman.

Just as Albert begins to align himself with Gandhi and King, the notes of the "*Twin Peaks* Theme" start to play in the background, and its volume rises as his speech approaches its climax. This music indicates our entrance into a fantasy space beyond the realm of everyday life. At this point, the series immerses us fully in the world of fantasy. This fantasy space renders Albert's profession of love believable.

Albert is one of the many idiosyncratic secondary characters that populate the first two seasons. His constant denigrations of rural life in Twin Peaks contrasts with Cooper's idealisation of it, but he doesn't play a central role in the events that transpire. Like Andy or Deputy Hawk (Michael Horse), Albert exists in the background. But in this position, he reveals the possibilities that the immersion in the fantasy world of *Twin Peaks* enable. There are many moments like Albert's profession of love for Sheriff Truman in the first two seasons of *Twin Peaks*, almost all of them signalled by the appearance on the audio track of Angelo Badalamenti's "*Twin Peaks* Theme".

Wally's appearance offers the opportunity for the type of connection that we see between Albert and Harry in the second season. But in *The Return*, the possibility for such connections no longer exists. When Sheriff Frank Truman (Robert Forster) comes out of the police station, he walks to Wally standing astride his motorcycle mimicking Marlon Brando in László Benedek's *The Wild One* (1953). Although Wally proclaims his connection to Sheriff Truman and the town of Twin Peaks, the scene makes clear the distance that separates them. The more that Wally accentuates the bond between Twin Peaks and himself, the more the estrangement becomes evident. Each time that Wally and Frank speak, Lynch includes a long silence that indicates this estrangement. Wally tells Frank "You know, my heart is always here with you and these fine people, my parents, who I love so dearly, and I was in the area, and I wanted to pay my respects". Although Frank expresses his thanks, Lynch includes a protracted period of silence before he speaks, and then cuts back and forth between shots of Wally and Frank looking awkwardly without speaking, before Wally resumes speaking. It seems as if neither Frank nor Wally knows how to respond to each other. This is because they lack the substrate of fantasy that not only makes such interactions possible but that enables a sublime moment to emerge, which is what we see occurring between Albert and Harry.

As he prepares to depart, Wally launches into a final statement that contrasts pointedly with Albert's profession of non-violence and love. Wally states:

> My family, my friend, I have criss-crossed this great land of ours countless times. I hold a map of it here, in my heart, next to the

> joyful memories of the carefree days I spent as a young boy here in your beautiful town of Twin Peaks. From Alexandria, Virginia, to Stockton, California, I think about Lewis and his friend Clark, the first Caucasians to see this part of the world. Their footsteps have been the highways and byways of my days on the road. My shadow is always with me, sometimes ahead, sometimes behind, sometimes to the left or sometimes to the right, except on cloudy days or at night.

As Wally speaks, the camera remains on him without cutting. We never see Frank's reaction, nor does the "*Twin Peaks* Theme" begin to softly rise to indicate their connection with each other. When Wally finishes speaking and the camera cuts to Frank, he simply stares at Wally, as if in disbelief. Frank wishes him well and walks back into the station.

The appearance of Wally Brando in episode four of *The Return* contributes nothing to the show's narrative, and he never reappears. His appearance does, however, illustrate how far removed we are in season three from the earlier seasons. As much as it might be tempting to see Wally as yet another quirky character produced by the *Twin Peaks* world, he is actually an index of how much this world has changed. In the same way, the death of the Log Lady (Catherine Coulson) in *The Return* indicates that we have left the world of fantasy for a barren world without any coordinates for mapping the path that our desire should take. Although she never seems connected to reality, her status as a fantasy figure in the first two seasons ensures the coherence of the *Twin Peaks* world, a coherence absent in *The Return*. Her cryptic messages to Deputy Hawk before her death indicate her absence from this world. This situation doesn't change until Agent Cooper reawakens in episode sixteen, and the fantasy world resumes.

Cooper's project

Dale Cooper's return is not the end of the fantasy in *The Return*. It is the beginning of it. The fantasy further includes the prevention of Laura Palmer's murder, the defeat of the figure of phallic enjoyment BOB, and the attempted triumph over the enigmatic negative force of Joudy.[5] The ultimate dream of the law is to prevent crimes before they happen rather than investigating them after the fact. The most effective police force would eliminate the need for its own policing power if it could do away with criminality before it comes into existence. Unfortunately, this dream requires the nightmare of a total surveillance state that would be worse than the crimes such a state would prevent. Many films deal with this nightmare and reveal its ramifications, like Wim Wenders' *The End of Violence* (1997) or Steven Spielberg's *Minority Report* (2002). In these films, the surveillance necessary for the prevention of crime creates an inhospitable social order that proves not worth the cost. In *Twin Peaks: The Return*, Dale Cooper does not resort to mechanisms like total surveillance or predicting future crimes to ward off a murder. Instead, he returns to the past and alters it directly.

Using the key to his former room at the Great Northern Hotel, Dale returns to the night of the murder of Laura Palmer. Indicating that Dale looks on from the perspective of the future, we see the events depicted in colour in *Fire Walk With Me* transpire in black and white here. Laura sneaks out of her house to James Hurley (James Marshall) awaiting on his motorcycle. When they stop to talk and profess their love for each other, Dale appears in the distance. Just after his appearance, Laura screams as she glimpses him in the woods. Although she likely assumes that it is BOB, it is actually Dale, who has come to rescue her rather than assault or kill her.

After Laura leaves James at the stoplight (just as she does in *Fire Walk With Me*), she walks through the woods to the cabin where Leo, Jacques, and Ronette await. But Dale interrupts her. When she takes his hand, the image turns from black and white to colour. He tells her that he is taking her home, which, given the abuse that she suffers from her father, cannot possibly mean the Palmer household. As they begin to walk hand-in-hand, Lynch cuts to the events of the next morning. Pete Martell

---

[5] At the beginning of episode sixteen, Gordon Cole provides a long exposition to Albert and Tammy about Cooper's quest, along with Major Briggs and himself, for an ancient negative force known as Joudy and ultimately as Judy. Cooper's attempt to save Laura from BOB includes a plan to eliminate Joudy as well, according to Gordon. But this plan to eliminate negativity as such necessarily fails.

(Jack Nance) goes fishing as he would the day he finds Laura's body, but we see the body wrapped in plastic disappear on shore, indicating that Dale has successfully altered history and saved Laura from BOB.

Rather than cut directly back to Cooper's rescue attempt, the show interposes a scene of Sarah Palmer (Grace Zabriskie) grabbing Laura's portrait off a table, thrusting it to the ground, and repeatedly stabbing it with a broken bottle. The scene of her stabbing the portrait with the bottle appears fractured, as it repeats the same shot again and again while drawing attention to the fragmented editing. Clearly, Sarah acts here in a manner similar to Leland when he is BOB. Although she is not raping Laura, she is performing an existential violence on her.

The evidence that Sarah is not just attacking Laura's portrait but Laura herself occurs in the next scene. When Lynch cuts back to Dale leading Laura through the woods, all of a sudden we see Laura's hand vanish from Dale's as a scratching sound occurs on the audio track (the same sound that the Fireman alerted Dale to in the first episode). One moment Laura is there, and the next she is gone. Just after her disappearance, as Dale looks for her, we hear her scream in horror as the camera pans across the empty woods. Dale succeeds in rescuing Laura from death at the hands of her father only to serve her up to some other malevolent force, because the attempt to escape negativity altogether always goes awry.

In the final episode, Dale and Diane embark on a mysterious plan that leads them to cross into another reality after they travel 430 miles. In this reality, Dale becomes transformed, perhaps into the figure of Richard named by the Fireman. He is more aggressive and less the pure fantasmatic figure that he was when he initially returned. He finds himself in Odessa, Texas, where he locates a woman who looks like Laura Palmer named Carrie Page (Sheryl Lee). He drives her from Texas to Twin Peaks, where they go to her house that she doesn't recognise and that doesn't contain her parents.

When returning to the street in front of the house after finding someone else living there, Dale stumbles and asks "What year is it?" Just afterwards, a soft voice upstairs in the house says "Laura", which prompts Carrie Page to scream. The show then ends with a cut to black. Though it isn't at all clear what violence Dale has introduced Laura/Carrie to, it is clear that he has not saved her but rather helped to repeat her trauma.

Snatching her away prior to her murder prevents one trauma, but it has the effect of unleashing another.

The problem with Agent Cooper's quest is not that he is trying to lessen suffering in the world. The problem lies instead with his belief that he can eliminate trauma as such or rid the universe of its negative force. Trauma constitutes the subject as a subject. To eliminate trauma before it occurs or to eliminate all negative force in the universe is to attempt to do away with subjectivity as such, which is why it always ends up producing additional trauma rather than alleviating it. This is why Lynch uses *Twin Peaks: The Return* to expose the damage done by the Agent Cooper fantasy.

The happy couple

Though it plays a minor part in the overall structure, there is one narrative thread in season three that has a conventional conclusion and shows characters able to break out of a destructive repetition. This is the relationship between Big Ed (Everett McGill) and Norma (Peggy Lipton). Having lived with a thwarted love for decades, first because of Norma's husband Hank (Chris Mulkey) and then because of Ed's wife Nadine (Wendy Robie), the two high school lovers appear destined to remain apart despite the background of their enduring love for each other. When season three begins, it initially seems as if Norma and Ed are finally together. We see them sitting together at a table in the Double R Diner, and they appear to be a couple. But when Walter Lawford (Grant Goodeve) arrives and kisses Norma, it becomes apparent that Ed and Norma are not a couple.

Walter is a financier helping Norma create a series of diner franchises modelled on her Twin Peaks original. While she seems satisfied with him, it's clear that some of his interest in her stems from the business potential of her diners. Early in the season, he points out that the other franchises are more profitable than the original Double R Diner, a deficit due to the high costs and low prices at the original. He attempts to convince Norma to use cheaper ingredients and to charge more for the pies at her diner, ideas that cause Norma to baulk. Nonetheless, their romantic relationship seems unaffected by these business differences. The prospects for Ed and Norma finally becoming a couple seem dim.

At the beginning of episode fifteen, however, events dramatically change. The episode starts with Nadine walking along the edge of the road carrying a golden shovel on her shoulder. She walks miles from her home to Ed's Gas Farm, where Ed is in the process of pumping gas for a customer when she arrives. Shocked that she walked the distance rather than driving, Ed is puzzled by her presence. After telling her about her love for him, she confesses, "I've been a selfish bitch to you all these years, and you've been a saint". She even avows her manipulation and use of guilt to coerce Ed into staying with her despite his love for Norma. Though Ed demurs, he eventually recognises that Nadine is finally telling him the truth.

Nadine credits her awakening to the webcast she has been watching created by Dr Jacoby (Russ Tamblyn) posing as Dr Amp. Jacoby proffers a blend of conspiracy theory and self-help that helps to drive Jerry Horne (David Patrick Kelly) into insanity, but that has a beneficent effect on Nadine. For $29.99 plus shipping, Nadine buys one of the golden shovels that Jacoby hawks so that she can, as she says, "shovel myself out of the shit". Just before she walks away, Nadine tells him that he is now free and that he should, "Go and enjoy". Ed looks dumbfounded but does eventually go to Norma in the diner.

It is significant that the prompt for Nadine's transformation originates with the conspiracy show and the spray-painted golden shovel from Dr Jacoby. Though the change is genuine, it has a fantasmatic origin. Purchasing a golden shovel is certainly not the key to honesty. Yet in the case of Nadine it does function as the instrument for freedom from her own self-deception. By allowing Dr Jacoby's programme to seduce her, Nadine breaks from the reality that had governed her existence for more than twenty-five years. Her honesty is not the product of stripping away the logic of fantasy, but of going deeper into it with the aid of Dr Jacoby.

When she grants Ed his freedom, he goes immediately to the Double R Diner to declare his love and availability to Norma. As Otis Redding's "I've Been Loving You Too Long" plays, we see Ed drive up in a golden truck (matching the colour of Nadine's shovel). When he enters, he waves joyfully at Norma and walks to her, proclaiming, "Norma, everything's changed. I just spoke with Nadine. She's given me her freedom". As he speaks, we see Walter walking towards the couple from behind Ed. Rather than instantly embracing him, Norma responds, "Ed, I'm so sorry. Walter's here". Norma and Walter walk to a table together to talk, with Ed seemingly left in the lurch at the counter (where he orders coffee and, under his breath, a cyanide tablet). Lynch ends this interaction with a clear indication that Ed has waited too long and that Norma's involvement with Walter precludes their reunion.

But this apparent rejection is not antithetical to the reunion. It is constitutive of it. Norma and Ed reunite not by overcoming the past and establishing a perfect complementarity. In order to enjoy the reunion of Ed and Norma, the spectator must first experience the lack at the heart of their relationship that Norma's initial apparent rejection indicates. Norma's conversation with Walter further establishes the logic of the subsequent relationship with Ed.

After Norma seems to reject Ed in favour of Walter, she sits down to discuss business with Walter. Through this discussion, Norma occasions a break with Walter that creates the opening for her return to Ed. Over Walter's strenuous objections, she tells him that she will divest from all the other franchises and focus her attention on the original Double R Diner. Norma's divestment from the process of accumulating capital puts off Walter, who angrily leaves after telling Norma that she is making a grave mistake. But this divestment makes it possible for her to proclaim her love for Ed and to accept his proposal.

The show interposes this gesture of divestment between Ed's initial proposal and Norma's acceptance not just to generate suspense but also to indicate the contrast between accumulation and love. There is a gap in the love relationship, like the gap that separates Ed's declaration of love from Norma's acceptance. The genuine love relation is possible only if the subjects involved are not seeking out what will complete them, as one is when one accumulates, which is why love and capitalism are fundamentally incompatible.

The relationship between Ed and Norma becomes possible because Norma's gesture reveals an acceptance of a fundamental incompleteness or lack that the other characters are unable to avow. The most important contrast with Norma is Dale Cooper. Lynch includes this sequence of Norma and Ed's reunion not just to please devoted fans of the show but to illustrate an alternative to the path that Dale chooses. Although Dale is no arch-capitalist, he commits himself fully to the project of eliminating loss completely by returning to the past to rescue Laura (and by defeating the evil forces of BOB and Joudy). What Lynch shows is that it is only through the acceptance of a fundamental loss that we can find a pathway to the satisfaction that we otherwise overlook.

The series doesn't end with Norma and Ed but with Dale's attempted fantasmatic rescue of Laura Palmer. The problem doesn't lie in the turn to fantasy itself—Norma and Ed are certainly ensconced in a fantasy—but in the belief of a restored harmony contained within the fantasy. Even as Dale saves Laura from the phallic enjoyment of BOB, he leaves the enjoyment of the drive signalled by Joudy operative. His attempt to eliminate Joudy has the effect of furthering the trauma of negativity rather than curtailing it, as Dale intends. This negativity returns in a repetition that we cannot eliminate but must comport ourselves towards. The actual return in *The Return* occurs at the end, with Cooper's failure to save Laura from negativity as such.

References

Frost, M. (2016). *The Secret History of Twin Peaks: A Novel.* New York, NY: Flatiron Books.

Geraghty, J. (2017). Insurmountable *Peaks. National Review*, 15 September. https://www.nationalreview.com/2017/09/twin-peaks-return-david-lynch-mark-frost-showtime-revival-disappoints-fans/.

Lacan, J. (2019). *The Seminar of Jacques Lacan, Book VI: Desire and Its Interpretation.* Cambridge: Polity.

McGowan, T. (2007). *The Impossible David Lynch.* New York, NY: Columbia University Press.

Nasio, J.-D. (2005). *Le Fantasme: Le plasir de lire Lacan.* Paris: Petite Bibliothèque Payot.

CHAPTER 11

Panel discussion on *Twin Peaks: The Return*

Chaired by *Jaice Sara Titus*

Tamara Dellutri, Richard Martin, Allister Mactaggart, and Todd McGowan

Editors' note

In addition to Richard Martin, Allister Mactaggart, and Todd McGowan, all of whom had discussed The Return *in their respective papers, this final panel of the conference also included psychoanalyst Tamara Dellutri, to whom we had assigned the task of watching* The Return *in its entirety in the space of a week, without having seen the previous seasons or* Fire Walk With Me. *We were interested to see what kinds of readings of* The Return *could emerge in the absence of any in-depth contextual knowledge of the* Twin Peaks *universe, readings that would not have recourse to the series' mythology and which might be less encumbered by the task of sense-making. The discussion opens with Dellutri's response to* The Return.

Tamara Dellutri:

I will first talk about the experience of watching *The Return* as an outsider. This, after all, is the challenge of a psychoanalyst: to listen to someone you haven't met before. You weren't there when things happened to those who consult you; all you have is what they are addressing to you.

This requires a mode of listening that suspends the temptation to decipher the narrative exclusively at the level of meaning, in order to give space to the question of the relation a given person has to meaning.

Freud and Lacan invite us to listen in a different way. There are various questions that are of interest to a psychoanalyst—for instance, the questions of:

- *Repetition*—What repeats, what is the impasse that insists?
- *Function*—What function does this or that peculiar construction have for this particular subject?
- *Visibility*—What is disclosed and what is hidden in a given speech act? Where does narrative consistency fragment?
- *Position*—What place does a given person assume in the Other of language?
- *Drive and enjoyment*—How is the body implicated when a person tells you their story? In which rim of the body does the drama unfold? For instance, someone's world might be organised primarily around the way they are looked at, while for someone else what matters most could be what they say (or cannot say) and what they are being told.
- *Excitation in speech*—The charges in a given speech: pitch, rhythms, accentuation, etc. What is the musicality a person makes when talking? What signifiers anguish a person and what pacifies their anxieties?

Analytic listening involves attending to an unknown narrative from an unusual perspective. Thus, when I sat to watch *The Return*, I asked myself what such a detached place of listening would add to the discussion. I will give you some brief context of my spectatorial experience, and then I will talk you through my thoughts.

I am an outsider not only to *Twin Peaks* but also to the screen culture of my generation. I was born on the outskirts of Buenos Aires and grew up in the pre-internet era during a prolific boom in the South American soap opera productions, which were deemed beneath the standards expected of my siblings and I at home. We did not have a TV, yet I spent precious hours of my youth peering through the window of the house next door, which had a giant TV screen that was visible from the pavement. That window frame where my sister and I spent intense fragmented hours is the foundation of my contact with TV productions and the bizarre spectatorial enjoyment that they provoke.

The opening episode of *The Return* evokes this mystique of the TV as an object. A couple are seated before a mysterious and forbidden (and thus eroticised) glass box. The couple is aroused under the object's watch, unaware of the imminent danger. As spectators we are invited to enjoy the couple's enjoyment, a fact that contrasts sharply with the closing minutes of the series finale, which echo in reverse the opening scenes of the series. If the inaugural episode features a couple brutally and mysteriously murdered by the intrusion from a glass box, the finale recapitulates a couple whose fantasy screen unexpectedly collapses, except that now it is the spectator who is deprived, unapologetically confronted with a scream and the empty visual field of a glass box. My first impression is that *The Return* builds up a narrative around an apparent excess of messages to be obtained, only to leave the spectator suddenly deprived of them. Neither clarifying nor resolving, the narrative ends with a sudden cut—a brute suspension of the spectator's scopic enjoyment.

As a psychoanalyst, I find Lynch to be a lucid and down-to-earth observer of the discrete, unique, and morbid ways in which bodies enjoy. There is nothing in Lynch that could indicate a standard of normality or a "normal world" even when his films attempt a depiction of a random town. Lynch is sensitive to the question of what fixes people's bodies to this or that, the question of what drives a body. This curiosity is not only present in the construction of his characters but also when considering the place of the spectator, specifically what Lacan, drawing on Freud's concept of the drive, calls the "scopic" and "invocatory" drives and their respective objects, the gaze and the voice, which are especially relevant to film production. I am referring here to the word Lacan chose to name the field of his clinical interest: jouissance, a word often translated as "enjoyment" but which we must not confuse with the word "pleasure". In fact, jouissance names a beyond of pleasure, an excess of excitation that is produced as a result of the curvature of language's structure upon the flesh of mortal beings.

Lynch shares with Freud and Lacan a concern around the *singular* in the subject, a concept that we must distinguish from the self or the individual or any form of subjective "niche" as it is often framed by neoliberal programmes of self-improvement. The singular is always implicated in the material causes of a subject as opposed to the points of identification. Lynch's curiosity is always engaged with the discrete singular features that emerge as what Lacanian psychoanalysis takes to be the result of each subject's traumatic and contingent encounter with the Other of language. This aperture allows him a candid, raw, and non-judgemental approach to different forms of existence. The only common denominator in Lynch's work is in fact the bizarre, often tinted with this unsettling, ominous dimension, a feature that gives over to singularity as such, inasmuch as what is singular to a given subject is radically and unavoidably foreign to others, and thus often received with disgust or wonder. Moreover, the marks that inhabit a given subject are often foreign to their own consciousness, provoking surprise when pointed out by loved ones, poked at by enemies, or suddenly discovered in the course of an analysis. This intimate invisibility is well captured by Freud's well-known observation that "the ego is not master in its own house". I find that the characters Lynch chooses to dialogue with in his films depict a common sensibility with key points in Freud and Lacan's work.

Richard Martin:

Tamara, your experience of watching the series is unique and so interesting. I have a couple of immediate thoughts. The first concerns soap operas. Of course, the original *Twin Peaks* has a parody within it, a soap opera called *Invitation to Love*. I've been thinking: what makes it impossible to have *Invitation to Love* in *The Return*? It just couldn't sit within the new series. What is it about *The Return* that makes it impossible to have a parody within it?

The second point relates to your comment about a universe with an excess of meaning. *The Return* is eighteen hours of conversations that *seem* to be meaningful, but are in fact full of failures of communication, messages that fail to be transmitted correctly. The entire series is orchestrated around media—Skype calls, text messages, coordinates for maps, intercoms, buzzers, entry systems—and all these things have glitches. No one seems able to communicate quite what they mean. I'm really interested in thinking about what it might mean for a series to be organised around the faulty transmission of messages.

Todd McGowan:

I want to touch on that question as well. The message that often fails in *The Return* does so because it has an excess attached to it. The meaning disappears beneath the excess of the form or the formal flourishes. This dynamic also exists between the series and the spectator. The appearance of Wally Brando, who seems to have no thematic purpose in the series at all, functions as an excessive signifier. He is there and signifies nothing at all. When people laugh at him, I think that they are laughing at this pure excess that also marks a failure in the series. It simply doesn't come off. To this end, I'm not sure that we could imagine a Wally Brando in the original *Twin Peaks*. Wally is excessive but signifies nothing, in contrast to the figures of excess from the first two seasons.

The Log Lady is one of the great figures of excess from the first two seasons, which is why I think Lynch chose her to introduce each episode when he re-released them. But she is so fundamentally different from Wally Brando. In this season, she's dying not only on the series but also in reality (which makes her scenes quite difficult to watch). What she's saying is never clear, but she's a figure of excess. Is she like Wally Brando or not? It seems to me that they're different. The space for him is now there but not for her. Her excess is an excess of meaning—there is always more meaning in what she says than what we can make out—while his is purely formal. He is excessive performance without signifying anything. The trajectory from the Log Lady to Wally Brando reveals how excess has dramatically changed. Excess is now completely wrapped up in performance.

Richard Martin:

I imagine we could have a whole panel discussion about Wally.

Todd McGowan:

Everyone hated that scene! People just turned it off and said "Michael Cera should kill himself!" But he read it, and it was funny. It was good.

Richard Martin:

Perhaps it's like the key scene in *Mulholland Drive*, where Betty performs a banal script with incredible intensity. I think embarrassment is the key word here. When Wally appears, I was embarrassed. I thought: "This is a kind of hipster intervention. It's too self-confident, it's exactly what we all want, it's ironic. And what a joke that these parents would produce this child".

But there's something else going on with embarrassment, which is really interesting, and that's the extent to which Lynch is able and prepared to risk his own embarrassment. I think this links nicely to the question earlier in the conference about the crudity of Lynch's special effects. Lynch doesn't want a smooth sheen, an easy viewing experience. He's prepared to risk something, and sometimes that involves vulgarity, perversion, or embarrassment. But at other times, it involves sincerity. There's a kind of wrenching sincerity to Lynch's work.

If we'd been sat in this space twenty-five years ago, the word that would have come up over and over again is "postmodern"—a sense that Lynch's work is all about pastiche and irony. But that discourse has disappeared because Lynch seems so authentic and so sincere, and Wally is part of that sincerity.

Allister Mactaggart:

A nice coincidence that we have our own special agent Tamara here, and the fact that she has come into *The Return* without having seen the other two immediately evokes Tammy Preston.

I'd like to pick up on what Richard was saying about failed communication. What suddenly struck me when you said that is that there is this scene in part six where Janey-E goes up to the people Dougie owes money to and gives this fantastic diatribe about contemporary capitalism. It struck me as a scene where there's very effective communication. She'd found out that Dougie made a bet for $20,000 and with interest the debt had grown exponentially to $52,000. She argues that as a member of the ninety-nine per cent of the population, they cannot afford this rate of interest, but offers instead twenty-five per cent interest upon the original loan, which she points out is much more than the minimal interest rate provided by her bank. They stand there looking very bemused and mutter that "she's a tough dame" as she walks away to her car, having non-negotiably made her deal with them, and then we go back into these scenes where we don't have those forms of communication.

There appears to be a theme about contemporary capitalism, or as I would call it, casino capitalism, that runs through *The Return*. It doesn't appear to be too overtly a critique, but we have a number of key scenes that revolve around money. Firstly, Dougie's mega wins in the Mustang Casino, then Janey-E sorting out Dougie's loan sharks, Dougie uncovering the insurance frauds followed by the repaying of money to the Mitchum brothers—who humorously change from being tough gangsters who beat up the casino manager for allowing Dougie's thirty mega wins to being people with "hearts of gold" in Cooper's eyes later on. Money and the effects of having/not having it seems to be a golden thread running through this season.

I keep away from social media and I was really worried about *The Return*. I got the box set and watched it over the Christmas period. I watched a couple of episodes a day and it was really disjointed. But when I went back to each episode and had the time to savour the images, to really think about the connections, the numbers, there's something really interesting about Lynch's relation to long-form television in an era of binge-watching: that this is a series where you have to take your time. That slowing of everything down demands something different from us, which goes against the grain of so much of what you watch. And you watch the next thing and you forget what you just watched, and there's a kind of cultural amnesia, whereas I think with Lynch there's something, perhaps related to his artwork, where he wants you to watch and to listen to the signifiers, to see the images, to play, and to actually let them resonate. And I think that is something that's unique in televisual format.

Todd McGowan:

Allister's point about the thematising of contemporary capitalism in *The Return* is important and helps to distinguish the third season from the earlier ones. In the first two seasons, the town of Twin Peaks seems isolated from contemporary capitalism. Ben Horne is, of course, a figure of capitalism, but he is very much a small-time and small-town capitalist.

But in season three, we are thrust into the heart of big capital in New York and Las Vegas. It even invades Twin Peaks as the Double R Diner spawns franchises. The only discussion we hear about them concerns how much profit they turn.

While *The Return* does present this critique of contemporary capitalism not present in the earlier seasons, it nonetheless reveals how the evil of Mr C trumps the logic of capital. I think that this is a very important idea for Lynch. Capitalism is never for him the ultimate evil. When capitalists try to use this evil in order to maximise profits, they typically end up destroyed by it, because the evil follows its logic and not that of capital. When capitalists think they are using Mr C, he is always really using them. And I would say that this is always true of diabolical evil like his.

Tamara Dellutri:

You have to bear in mind that I watched the entire series in a week. It is my impression that *The Return* operates on the spectator a certain demand for deciphering. Why is that? Everything seems to have a given meaning; there is a sense that whatever happens to Cooper, whatever colour he looks at, it means something. It seems to me that the format in which the narrative is organised, always around points of suspense, tension, and mysterious signals, has something to do with this effect: spectators find themselves presupposing knowledge all the time. We were discussing this yesterday: how on social media people started to produce more meaning, more interpretations. People thought the flickering windows of the FBI jet was some sort of code, or ran the sound playing from the gramophone through sound analysers in search of some truth. The twist though is, as you have both noted, that these "signs" often lead nowhere. Lynch creates a narrative that invites the spectator to fill up the gaps in meaning with "turf of their own", a narrative that seems loaded with messages to be deducted but ultimately unravels itself as one with no purpose. I really adore this nuance. I find this feature particularly "playful" in the Lacanian sense of the expression.

Todd McGowan:

That's right, there was a wild flurry of meaning-making—but I want to pick up on the idea of the *missed* communication. It's a tiny detail, but Bushnell Mullins had the Mitchum brothers on speed dial! Rather than suggesting a connection, it indicates a kind of disjunction. Even in the Twin Peaks Sheriff's Office with the computer screen that comes out of the desk. There's a whole elaborate mechanism for communication, and yet none of the communication comes off without a hitch. There's a constant communication disjunction, and I'd link that back to the production of meaning by everyone in response to the show. No one in the show connects at the level of the signifier, but then you get this audience saying, "I have to make sense of it". The desperate attempts at meaning-making are the response to the failure of communication. The enjoyment (or boredom) of the signifier has completely eclipsed any signification.

Tamara Dellutri:

The tendency towards sense-making also assumes that messages always arrive at a point of the meaning intended, whereas in fact messages are most of the time broken. The Freudian discovery of the unconscious implies that the statement and point of enunciation of a given message are not aligned. A fact we are reminded of when a well-intended message comes back to us in unexpected albeit monstrous forms.

Todd McGowan:

That's what I was just going to say. I don't think there finally is an essence to be deciphered, and that's why the code from the jet, or the music analysis, and all that stuff is a response to what the show is more about, which is the failure of meaning.

Richard Martin:

And that the production of meaning is always mediated. One of the skills that Evil Cooper has is that he's a tech genius. He can hack things in a way that's totally unrealistic, and this draws attention to the fact that everything is being mediated; everything is going through forms of transmission, encoding, modes of ciphering. The production of further theories and additional meanings often aims at an ideal, at a purity of meaning, whereas all the messages in *The Return* are mediated, grubby, and full of glitches.

Allister Mactaggart:

That made me think of when Lucy goes in and shoots Evil Cooper and says "now I understand mobile phones".

Audience question:

I wanted to invite Tamara to reflect on the scene where Richard Horne kills the child. We discussed it earlier and you had a wonderful take on it.

Tamara Dellutri:

Why is that scene so intense? I think it operates a little collapse of the distance between the signifier and the materiality of the world. A collapse (in the reality of the character) of the metaphorical function of language provokes a literalisation, which is evocative of the logic of psychosis. In the previous scene, Richard Horne is confronted with Red, who intimidates him, and we witness a scene that is a sort of castration for Richard. His boss calls him a "kid" while he flips a coin in the air, which makes me think of Lacan's famous *vel* of alienation: "your money or your life". Richard is forced into a choice that unavoidably confronts him with a loss that is unbearable for him to assume. This impossibility is brilliantly depicted in the montage of the events. There is a displacement operated by the narrative: Richard cannot (symbolically or materially) kill this "father-boss" who humiliates him so unbearably, this man who puts an unexpected limit on him. The realisation of his own position as the child in relation to this man is unendurable to him. He cannot bear the "kid" in himself, but neither can he efface it. The image he has created of himself is destroyed by this father-boss and he cannot deal with it. Out of the unbound anger this humiliation provokes in him, Richard unwittingly runs over a child who happens to cross the road while he is driving.

I find this literalisation of the internal violence the character struggles with a majestic rendering on Lynch's part. It is a brutal and traumatic scene. In my view, the scene's crudity is widened by the effect of this collapse of the boss's word "kid" into the actual killing of a kid on the road. The loss of distance between what is implied and what materially happens in the reality of Horne's life is horrific, and the fact that this loss of distance is provoked by a contingency—a random kid crossing the street—makes the scene even more powerful. This form of collapse between the signifier and the world is often present in the experience of psychosis.

Allister Mactaggart:

There's also money again at the heart of this scene. Red flicks a coin into the air, which magically reappears in Richard's mouth and then in Red's hand. The link between money and power reappears in another guise here. Richard's humiliation, anger, and impotence at being called "kid" leads directly to the actual killing of a young kid in what is a terribly moving scene, as Tamara says. What is unbearable for Richard becomes unbearable for the people who witness the killing, and also terribly moving for us as viewers.

Todd McGowan:

That's exactly right. To put it in psychoanalytic terms, the idea is that one's inability to accept one's castration leads directly to violence. Richard confronts his castration, recoils, and then acts out in what is probably the most difficult scene of the series to watch. Its unwatchability—I have almost turned away each time I've rewatched the series—stems from the sense that we know what's coming. And we know what's coming because we have seen that Richard has endured, or failed to endure, this insult.

Audience question:

I was wondering to what extent there might be a link between the mysterious nightmarish figure behind Winkie's Diner in *Mulholland Drive* and the Woodsmen in *The Return* who seem to bring BOB back to life. They seem to have a similar quality. Any thoughts?

Richard Martin:

My immediate response is that there's something very interesting but also problematic in the kind of literalisation process that Lynch often uses—where there's an abstract fear and then it literalises in the world.

In the *Mulholland Drive* scene, the thing that Diane fears most is the back alley, behind the glamour of Hollywood, the place where dreams end, which is also a form of homelessness. What Lynch gives us is a ridiculously stereotyped, homeless, scary figure. This is both interesting—because it links with that "crudity" and "embarrassment" we discussed before—but problematic as well.

I'm not sure if the same logic applies to the Woodsmen. But we could see them as a literalisation of evil, of what emerged from the Atomic Bomb.

Todd McGowan:

One difference is that I don't think the figure behind Winkie's speaks. I think what's disturbing about the Woodsmen is their constant repetition of the same phrase: first, it's "gotta light?" and then it's the poem about the water and the well. As a spectator, I found this incredibly annoying. I just wanted them to stop saying that when I was watching it, and I think that's how you're supposed to react (I always take how I react as how you're supposed to react, which may be a problem!).

To me, the attack of the Woodsmen was an instance of what Tamara was talking about earlier—the voice as object. Their voice becomes completely disconnected from the realm of meaning. We experience the trauma of the voice as the object replete with enjoyment and thus threatening to overwhelm us. I find the scene behind Winkie's operating much more on the visual field. It's like when you see someone out of your ordinary life, it's fine, as long as they don't say something to you. Once they speak, then it's traumatic. So it seems to me that the Woodsmen are more traumatic than the guy behind Winkie's.

Richard Martin:

Do you mean the Žižekian idea that they come too close?

Todd McGowan:

Yes, of course, they're too close. I thought they were going to kill everyone that they saw. They're right in the face of everyone with whom they come into contact. I think that's in some way the difference between gaze and voice. The voice is *invading* you, whereas gaze can be traumatic—you're identified with it so you're out of yourself—but nonetheless there is some physical distance from what you confront.

Tamara Dellutri:

Yes, I agree with Todd. It is curious that Lacan seems to see in the voice a supportive function that is unparalleled by other objects. It is not insignificant that Lacan uses the voice as opposed to the gaze in order to name the dimension of the drive in the elaborations of his graph of desire.

As Todd points out, when the voice turns back on us, its intrusion is devastating; clinically, we are aware of the intrusion of the voice in some presentations of psychosis. The subject's own voice has no shield to hide the emergence of affect. The voice has a relation to anxiety that the gaze hasn't: the voice doesn't lie. As Lacan pointed out, we can close our eyes but we cannot close our ears: there is nothing in the subject's anatomy that puts a limit on the voice of others. Perhaps it is this structural precariousness and powerless relation a subject has to the voice—their own and the Other's—that makes Lacan (and Lynch) choose the voice as a privileged object.

Todd McGowan:

Right. There's something more traumatic and invasive about voice. This is why I think that the Woodsmen sequence resonates so much with viewers, and is one reason why so many people love episode eight.

Audience question:

Something I feel has been alluded to but not directly expressed is Lynch as an American director who is concerned with specifically American subjectivity. In relation to *The Return*, there seems to be a moment in American rhetoric now of "Make America Great Again". Talking about *The Shape of Water*, Guillermo del Toro recently described the 1950s as "the America people mean when they say 'Make America Great Again' ". I feel like the "Gotta Light?" episode articulates a desire to return to a fantasy space of America that never really existed, and creates this as an entanglement of the site of trauma and the site of desire. So what does the panel think about how *The Return* specifically positions American subjectivity *now*?

Allister Mactaggart:

That's a really interesting question. There's a bit in the extras where he's showing the scene with the Woodsman going into the radio station, and one of the things Lynch keeps saying is "it was much darker in the 1950s! Much darker! Much darker!". And in his own personal biography, going back into the 1980s, if we were saying that twenty odd years ago, that the discourse was postmodernity and being very reductive about these figures, there was this question of whether Lynch is a conservative, what he said about Ronald Reagan, and then we look at the figure of the Cowboy in *Mulholland Drive*.

This is veering into some speculative ideas about his biography, but I think there is that sense that *The Return* is looking back to the 1950s and trying to find a point of significant change that happened around that time. I mean, he said that there was a time when industry and nature seemed to be working in conjunction and everything appeared to be fine, but then we realised it was going wrong. And I think in *The Return* he's going back to think about it, but actually to think about all the complexity that was happening then. That it wasn't a time that was ever fantastic—that's a myth, a fantasy. How do we read the Trinity test? In the series it becomes a kind of origin myth, but I think it's a much more complex, nuanced relationship to what was going on in America. Going back to Richard's paper, Richard was talking about the responses to that test in geographical terms with the domes, and then the expanded highway system, which was a way of taking weapons all over the country, and now we have a situation where we don't have that, we have the sprawl that you see in *The Return*. So what does that say about America now, about America's response to world events? Is it a sense of all the things Trump says about America's position? But actually you've got a paradox between that of various forms of enclosure, which contrast against a sprawl that goes outwards. And is he saying that there's not much we can do about this, or showing fear or anxiety? I think Lynch is grappling with that, and I think it shows a great maturity in the work that there's no easy answer about how it could relate to contemporary debates.

There seems to be a sense of Lynch's nuanced vision here relating to the distinction Svetlana Boym refers to between restorative nostalgia – which is nationalistic and prone to believing each and every conspiracy theory going—and reflective nostalgia, in which the past has a value for the present, for what was unrealised in the past. And this might link to Norma Jennings' decision to exercise her right to be bought out of the franchise she'd entered into since we were last in Twin Peaks, and return to owning just the one, original Double R Diner. In a sense, this can also be seen as a micro reflection upon neoliberalism in the intervening period and Norma's realisation of what is lost in the process of economic expansion. Accompanied by the emotional intensity of Otis Redding's live version of "I've Been Loving You Too Long", the resultant public display of Big Ed's and Norma's love for each other is a form of reflective nostalgia—a fulfilment of a previously unrealised future that the viewer also has been waiting for, for too long. But, at the same time as we have this vision of a beautifully resolved relationship, Lynch also always makes us aware of the other side of nostalgia—the dangerous underside which has been consistently present throughout his work.

Todd McGowan:

Right, the underside of nostalgia is always foregrounded in Lynch. His point is that if we want the benefits of how things were, we always have to pay the price. In a sense, Norma is willing to pay the price to return to her love with Ed. The price is abandoning her position as a fledgling capitalist. If she doesn't give up the franchises, then no reunion with Ed would be possible. At the end of the series, Cooper pays the price for wanting to return to a past in which Laura wasn't murdered. But unlike Norma, he doesn't believe he has to pay the price.

Richard Martin:

If we're going to talk about this in the context of Trump, and in a particularly urgent moment for racial politics, one of the ways that *The Return* is useful is that it's very much a text about whiteness.

Lynch's representation of race is often problematic. His worlds are almost totally white and when characters of colour do appear they're often framed in problematic ways—this is most evident in *Wild at Heart*. At the same time, he is extremely useful for thinking about the investments that are made in whiteness. We can think about how whiteness functions in Lumberton in *Blue Velvet*, how it underpins Laura Palmer's "innocence" in *Twin Peaks*, how in *Mulholland Drive* it supports Betty's conception of Los Angeles and how her fantasy might compare with the Hispanic history of LA.

With *The Return*, having eighteen hours of contemporary American television that is almost totally white provides—at this point in time—a very useful cultural text for examining what's invested in whiteness. I think this speaks directly to questions of contemporary American subjectivity.

Todd McGowan:

That's a great point and I want to say a couple of things, firstly, about race: I was fascinated by the Rancho Rosa billboard because if you were to drive around America, you would never ever see a billboard with all white people in it. Even though there are a lot of neighbourhoods that just have white people in them, the sign of the neighbourhood would always be multicultural or multi-ethnic.

The second thing is, I think it's fascinating that Lynch doesn't seem to think you can come home again. He's no Thomas Wolfe. You can go home again, but what you go back to was a pretty horrible thing. That "gotta light?" line is perfect. What was "gotta light?" That was stereotypically the way you articulated your investment in the social bond in the 1950s. But what's depicted here is horrible. No one in the universe of *The Return* would want to be approached with this phrase. The traditional phrase of the 1950s becomes the source of an incredible trauma. So I think what Lynch is saying is that the thing we have this nostalgia for—and he likes milkshakes, too—has this other, horrible underside to it. He's saying that you can't just have the one without the other. It is part of that "Make America Great Again" attitude, except he's saying that what it was was this horrible thing too. Perhaps this is the best possible response to the retrograde politics of our time.

Audience question:

Something that hasn't been massively discussed is the temporal shifts that keep happening through the series, which for me was the hook. Richard's paper on sprawl discussed this Hito Steyerl quote about "junk-time". When the superimposition of Cooper's face appears I found it to be one of the most traumatic moments, because for me it seemed like we'd just been watching in "junktime", watching all of this happening as Cooper's been observing, and now we're going to see really what's happening. And it kept happening—there's been a lot of commentary on scenes that flip—characters change clothes, people change places, every scene was terrifying from the timeline where Laura disappears and Leland has killed himself. So that reflection on time—going back in time and changes in time.

Todd McGowan:

The scene that immediately came to mind was the Sarah Palmer scene with the boxing match that repeats again and again. The boxing match repeats to the point that it begins to really grate on the spectator. And then a similar repetition occurs with Sarah Palmer destroying Laura's picture.

To me the whole show is about the way in which repetition functions. I don't think Lynch just thinks we're stuck in repetition and that's all there is—because why would you make a show if you thought that—but you have to in some way engage with that repetition and take stock of it, and you can't escape it totally. To me, that's what's underlying *The Return*. When you get a glitch of repetition in the actual scene, that's a synecdoche for what's going on in the whole series.

What I love the most about *The Return* is how it depicts the failure of our attempts to alter repetition. In a sense, this is the most basic claim that the series is making. Dale Cooper's *raison d'être* is to stop repetition. Maybe that's the function of the FBI as well. But the end of the series reveals that he absolutely fails. In the attempt to lift Laura out of the traumatic repetition that has defined her existence, he effectively reinserts her back into it. There is no respite from repetition. Freedom can only exist in the relationship that we take up to repetition, which is where I think the series is trying to intervene.

Richard Martin:

When Audrey started her characteristic "Audrey's dance", I thought: "this is really weird, it's a total pastiche, it's old *Twin Peaks*". But then, *snap*, it ends and she's somewhere else. It's a flip, two things going on at once, which might be linked to trauma and the dissociation of trauma.

Tamara Dellutri:

In the final cut, before the scene collapses, closing the series, there is a question about time: "what year is this?" There is a disassociation, a "pastiche" at the level of time. The spectator is confronted with this experience of rupture that citing Freud, Lacan defines as "*die idee einer anderer Lokalität*", "the idea of another locality, another space, another scene"; the "non-temporal locus" between perception and consciousness in which the unconscious manifests itself.

Richard Martin:

I would add that, as ever with Lynch, it's about media. The engagement with nostalgia in *Blue Velvet* or the original *Twin Peaks* is much smoother and warmer. What you get in the digital aesthetic of *Inland Empire* and *The Return* is harsher and sharper with an instant switch between different worlds, which reflects a twenty-first-century digital experience. We all have the ability to go from 1945 to 1956 to 1990 to 2017, to go backwards and forwards through cultural texts and references. In this respect, Lynch's recent work feels very different to the work he was making in the 1980s and 1990s, which had its own distinctive take on nostalgia.

Allister Mactaggart:

There's something really interesting about the glitch throughout the series. When Cooper falls out of the Red Room and he ends up in that purple building. All kinds of things are going on there—how it keeps breaking down, banging on the door—it's so much about digital technology, what it allows, but also what breaks down all the time. But at the same time throughout, there's this sense of Lynch and Frost wanting to keep the whole thing going, and some sort of conflict between having to come to an end even after eighteen episodes and wanting to keep it going again. In the *Special Dossier* by Mark Frost, there's a bit in Tamara Preston's report that says Laura Palmer didn't die on the day she disappeared, and then we go to part seventeen where she screams looking at Cooper when he's taking her along. On the one hand, you're thinking: please make it safe for Laura! But then where is this home? There's a complex relationship between having to finish, and also wanting to keep stories going and going, seeking to keep death at bay. And just within the series, thinking about the people who are no longer there, who actually died since *Twin Peaks* first came out. It's very hard to watch the Log Lady. There's all these people and you're thinking: "gosh, they're no longer with us!" They're on the tape, we can see them there, but there's a sadness you feel at the same time in wanting to continue, wanting to keep death at bay.

Tamara Dellutri:

It touches on a word we use a lot in psychoanalysis: "cut", the cut of the session, which as someone once said is like a *coitus interruptus*. The cut is, of course, also crucially relevant for the very construction of film, a reason for which it has been extensively theorised. In this opportunity, I thought about the function of the cut in the context of the praxis of psychoanalysis. If the discourse of the university entails the production of knowledge, the discourse of the analyst is concerned with a subversive manoeuvre: the disruption of a knowledge that is taken for granted.

It is my impression that in *The Return* Lynch constructs a scenario only to operate a disruption for his spectators which reminded me of the cut of the analytic session. A good cut of a session, when it occurs (because it does not very often), produces an effect of alienation that could be compared with a Brechtian *Verfremdungseffekt*. This is the unsettling moment where a cut in the narrative of a session can retrospectively highlight our own implication in the scene we have been denouncing to the analyst for ages. A good cut of the session can unveil the "ob-scene" we have been inadvertently involved with but conveniently left out. Lynch's use of the cut is particularly effective in the last scene of the series where, as I mentioned, he unexpectedly suspends the "joui-sense" (the excess of meaning production) with a sudden interruption that confronts the spectators to their own morbid position: they have been seated for hours and hours, watching something that ends in nothing. Inadvertently or not, Lynch confronts the spectator with their own waste: of time, of lucubration, of excitation—he really pokes into that useless, lazy enjoyment characteristic of conventional TV spectatorship.

Audience question:

Richard, your paper touches on the image of the Atomic Bomb, taking away a face value, a way of fragmenting, a destruction of meaning and order. To me, it was the Holocaust that epitomises the anguish he is expressing. And a mistrust of language: that we can never be at home in the symbolic order, that the uncanny is part of the human condition.

Richard Martin:

That's extremely interesting. I'm very wary of instrumentalising catastrophic historical events and thinking about them in simplistic ways in order to make sense of cultural texts. But I've often thought about the Holocaust in relation to *Inland Empire*, and I've heard other people say that too. Much of *Inland Empire* was shot in Łódź in Poland, a city that had an enormous Jewish population and then a notorious Jewish ghetto established by the Nazis. It's where two of Kafka's siblings were killed, and Lynch has often talked about Kafka as a "brother". There's a sense of deep trauma in *Inland Empire*, but what it does mean to think about Lynch's work at that level of historical calamity?

When it comes to *The Return*, I was in two minds about the Atomic Bomb in relation to the series' sprawling landscape, just as Todd is reluctant to read it straight. It seems too easy an answer. At the same time, if we think about Lynch's entire career as a project about the post-war world, the Bomb dropping in *The Return* feels like the origin of everything that has obsessed him: Eisenhower conservatism, the veneration of small-town America, white picket fences. And it leads on to Lynch's other engagements with American history: the Kennedy assassinations, Marilyn Monroe, Ronald Reagan, etc.

So, the Bomb dropping makes total sense to me within *The Return*—a work that clearly comes towards the end of Lynch's career—as a statement on the origin of the post-war world. But again, I'm wary of using an event of such historical enormity in a simplistic fashion.

Audience question:

I'd like to return to that theme of language and messages. It's significant that David Lynch's own character, Gordon Cole, is deaf; he has a hearing aid, and he can either turn up what he hears so it's really acute or take it out completely. Equally, sometimes as an audience we're literally leaning forward to hear what people are going to say. And sometimes we get characters where meaning seems to reach the edge of the word; they say something that seems to make everything bind together in a symbolic frame. For example, the character that appears as a floating head, that perhaps there's something that can never be said. Are there moments in Lynch's work where things *can* be said that mean what they say they mean?

Tamara Dellutri:

In a way you're touching on the question of enjoyment in speech. There is a spectrum in the series: from characters that cannot utter to characters that utter too loudly or just too much. A variety of modes of enjoying speech that addresses the materiality of speech as such. In Lynch's work, there are plenty of observations about the enjoyment that subjects derive in speaking. This is the difference between language and *lalangue*, the point where we verify that speaking is much more than the conveyance of messages: letters also have a jouissance value.

In a way, when I was referring to modes of speech I was referring to that variety, which for me has to do with the materiality of speech and the enjoyment in speech: this difference between language and *lalangue*. There is something about *lalangue* that is fascinating for Lynch, the enjoyment that there is in speaking as such.

Audience question:

I wanted to come back to this theme of nostalgia and how it relates to revivals and continuations and reboots. There seems to be a lot of ambivalence towards the very concept. Moments like with Audrey's dance are very nostalgic, but they're also the ones that are most fraught with danger. When Shelly, Bobby, and Becky are in the diner, where they're having their very soap opera family discussion, but then a gun goes off and it turns into something bizarre and dangerous. It seems like a way of commenting on a nostalgic longing to return to a safe, comfortable, warm space, which is actually impossible.

Allister Mactaggart:

And again, I think that's really interesting when we look at nostalgic returns across culture. Bands are reforming, Simon Reynolds has written about retromania in pop music. And there's nothing worse than bands getting back together and playing all their old albums live track by track, whereas I think Lynch is saying that although there's a desire to go back, there's also a fear. Be careful what you wish for! Nostalgia isn't what it used to be! It's as if he's saying: alright, let's go back and see what's happened. And what the series picks up on so well is what happened to America over that period. The Double R is now a franchise. It picks up on a lot of what happened in neoliberalism over that period. There's an acknowledgement of the desire to go back, but also a demonstration that when we go back we find something different.

Richard Martin:

I appreciate your question and I think we need to talk about Audrey. Lynch is extremely generous towards many of his returning characters. They're often presented in really warm ways, like Bobby, Ed, and Norma. Yet the treatment of Audrey is really perverse. There's a paper to be written called: "Waiting for Audrey". We're all waiting for her to get out of that room, and then finally she leaves only to end up in terrible limbo at the end. I've heard people suggest she's been sectioned. Certainly, something traumatic happens to her, and the way she's represented throughout the series tells us something about what Lynch wants to resist in terms of nostalgia: he won't give us the coffee, doughnuts, and cherry pie that we might expect. Audrey is for me the central figure here: why does he treat her the way he does?

Audience response:

I think it's partly because, as was said yesterday about Audrey as a style icon, she's become very emblematic of the show, so resisting showing her for so long almost feeds into that resistance to pure nostalgia.

Audience question:

Citing the geographic sprawl, it seems that there's also a mythological sprawl going on in *The Return*. From a giant who is localised within Twin Peaks we have him defined in what appears to be a kind of eternal force. And then we have, on the other side, Judy and the teapot formerly known as David Bowie. Is all this to be regarded as simply an excess of meaning or is there something else going on here that spurs discussion?

Todd McGowan:

This is where with Lynch's return to *Twin Peaks* there are certain contingencies of people dying or going crazy that necessitated him changing things. It does fit, but it allows him to fight against the nostalgia that drives much of the viewership of the series. Maybe it's true that there aren't any accidents. At the very least, Lynch manages to take these contingencies of people's deaths and other derailments in order to show—as Allister was saying—that there's both a giving in to the nostalgia and then also a revelation that what you actually get is not what you thought you were getting. In this sense, I think Richard is absolutely right that Audrey is the key figure. When we finally see her and her relationship, we get what we want as spectators and find that we don't want it. This is the perfect way to treat nostalgia.

I just wanted to say something about race. It's hard to read Lynch as a great anti-racist, but wouldn't it be totally crazy to say that the reason he doesn't focus on characters of colour is that what he's trying to really do is expose how nostalgia for white America is nostalgia for a pretty poisonous America, and he wants to show that it's a particularly white-inflected poison. It's too generous to him, but perhaps that's one line of defence tied to this nostalgia question. I don't ultimately think that this lets him off the hook on the question of racism. There are many problems in this regard, even in *The Return*. The figure of Jade, the black prostitute, for instance, is stereotypical.

Richard Martin:

In terms of mythology, there are times when *Twin Peaks* and *The Return* can seem very simple, despite all the elaborate storylines. The myth of Orpheus and Eurydice really frames Cooper's rescue act, and that myth is explicitly referenced in the penultimate episode of *The Return*.

Audience question:

I was wondering if you could comment on the role of dreaming and the insistence that we live inside a dream, and this question of "who is the dreamer?"

Tamara Dellutri:

My impression is that once we enter elucubrations about the "dream within the dream" we miss the point that Freud makes when he speaks about the "navel" of the dream: in principle the dream is not a never-ending production. The dream-work envelopes a hidden real, a limit-point, an impossible-to-represent (for a given subject). In *Seminar XI*, Lacan develops this theme in relation to the concept of *automaton* and *tuchē*, the mis-encounter with the real, and he makes a connection between this mis-encounter and waking up from a dream. In a playful interpretation I am tempted to take the final decomposing scream as an index of this "navel": a blind point where all possible narrative collapses and, as spectators, we are abruptly pushed to "wake up", so to speak.

Todd McGowan:

To me, what Lynch is trying to say is that the logic that governs our dreams often governs the way we experience our social reality as well. I think *The Return* does a great job of showing that, and I think Richard made some really insightful claims about the connections that are being made on the level of the narrative, which are not necessarily narratively linked but are associative connections, as in a dream. And to me, that's how we experience reality. You'll be thinking about something, and that's why you see something. And if you weren't thinking it, you wouldn't have seen it. So there's a sense in which we are living inside a dream all the time.

The ending really emphasises the dream logic of the entire series. It all ends with Laura's scream, which occurs at the moment when she recognises that she is caught up in a repetition that she cannot escape. The logic is one of association, just like the dream, but the association doesn't lead to the new. It instead always leads back to the force of repetition. What seems to have informed our entire discussion of *The Return* is the absolute priority of repetition in what occurs. The series proffers certain fantasies of escape, but even these fantasies lead back to the trauma of repetition. If we live inside a dream for Lynch, we live inside a structure that repeats, and we have to make our way through that repetition rather than imagining some type of escape from it.

Index